中国法院

的

司法改革

2013—2018

中华人民共和国最高人民法院

Judicial Reform of Chinese Courts

人民法院出版社

图书在版编目（CIP）数据

中国法院的司法改革. 2013—2018 / 中华人民共和国
最高人民法院编.— 北京：人民法院出版社, 2019.2

ISBN 978-7-5109-2447-7

Ⅰ. ①中… Ⅱ. ①中… Ⅲ. ①司法制度—体制改革—
研究—中国—2013-2018 Ⅳ. ①D926.04

中国版本图书馆CIP数据核字（2019）第033114号

中国法院的司法改革（2013—2018）

中华人民共和国最高人民法院　编

责任编辑　丁丽娜
出版发行　人民法院出版社
地　　址　北京市东城区东交民巷27号（100745）
电　　话　（010）67550608（责任编辑）　　67550558（发行部查询）
　　　　　　65223677（读者服务部）
客 服 QQ　2092078039
网　　址　http://www.courtbook.com.cn
E – mail　courtpress@sohu.com
印　　刷　三河市国英印务有限公司
经　　销　新华书店
开　　本　787×1092毫米　1/16
字　　数　145千字
印　　张　10.5
版　　次　2019年2月第1版　2019年2月第1次印刷
书　　号　ISBN 978-7-5109-2447-7
定　　价　38.00元

目　录

Contents

前　言

　　法治是治国理政的基本方式，司法是法治体系的重要基石。全面深化司法改革，对于完善和发展中国特色社会主义司法制度、促进国家治理体系和治理能力现代化，具有重大而深远的意义。2013 年以来，中国法院始终坚持立足中国国情，把握时代脉搏，以让人民群众在每一个司法案件中感受到公平正义为目标，坚定不移全面深化司法改革，人民法院审判执行工作全方位发展，司法效能、司法能力和司法公信全面提升，取得了丰硕成果。

一、中国法院制度和改革历程

中国法院改革的制度基础

根据《中华人民共和国宪法》和《中华人民共和国人民法院组织法》，人民法院作为国家的审判机关，依照法律规定独立行使审判权，不受行政机关、社会团体和个人的干涉。国家设立最高人民法院、地方各级人民法院和军事法院等专门人民法院。人民法院依照法律规定审理民事案件、刑事案件、行政案件以及法律规定的其他案件，开展民事执行、行政执行等司法活动。独任法官、合议庭、审判委员会和赔偿委员会是法律规定的审判组织。

最高人民法院是中华人民共和国最高审判机关，负责审理全国范围内有重大影响的或者法律规定由其审理的各类案件，制定司法解释，监督和指导地方各级人民法院和专门人民法院的审判工作，并依照法律确定的职责范围管理全国法院的部分司法行政工作。

地方各级人民法院包括基层人民法院、中级人民法院和高级人民法院。专门人民法院包括军事法院、海事法院、知识产权法院、金融法院等。

上级人民法院监督和指导下级人民法院的审判工作。在诉讼活动中，人民法院依法实行审判公开、合议、回避、人民陪审员、辩护、两审终审等制度。

中国法院改革的基本历程

改革开放以来，随着经济社会全面发展，民主法治不断进步，人民群众对司法的要求和期待日益增长，原有的司法体制已经不能适应形势发展的需要。早在 20 世纪 90 年代，中国法院就开始了以强化庭审功能、扩大审判公开、推进司法职业化建设为重点内容的改革历程。中国共产党第十五次全国代表大会以来，最高人民法院在法院组织体系、法官制度、诉讼程序、审判方式、执行制度、司法管理等方面，开展了一系列改革，并于 1999 年、2005 年、2009 年分别发布了三个"人民法院五年改革纲要"。这三个纲要是 2013 年之前中国法院改革的基本依据。

中国共产党第十八届中央委员会第三次全体会议通过的《中共中央关于全面深化改革若干重大问题的决定》，确定了推进法治中国建设、深化司法体制改革的重要任务。第十八届中央委员会第四次全体会议通过的《中共中央关于全面推进依法治国若干重大问题的决定》，将建设中国特色社会主义法治体系、建设社会主义法治国家确立为全面推进依法治国的总目标，从科学立法、严格执法、公正司法、全民守法等方面提出了一系列重大改革举措。司法改革成为中国全面深化改革的重要组成部分，被纳入国家整体发展战略。

为进一步深化人民法院各项改革，最高人民法院制定《关于全面深化人民法院改革的意见》，提出 65 项改革举措，并将之作为《人民法院第四个五年改革纲要(2014—2018)》,于 2015 年 2 月 4 日发布实施。截至 2018 年底,65 项改革任务已全面推开,涉及改革文件 256 件。其中,最高人民法院单独印发改革文件 173 件,会同中央有关部门印发 46 件,推动或参与制定 37 件。

中国共产党第十九次全国代表大会作出"深化司法体制综合配套改革，全面落实司法责任制，努力让人民群众在每一个司法案件中感受到公平正义"的重大战略部署，标志着深化司法体制改革进入新阶段。最高人民法院结合法院实际制定《关于深化人民法院司法体制综合配套改革的意见》，也即《人民法院第五个五年改革纲要（2019—2023）》，作为未来五年指导人民法院深化司法体制综合配套改革工作的重要纲领。

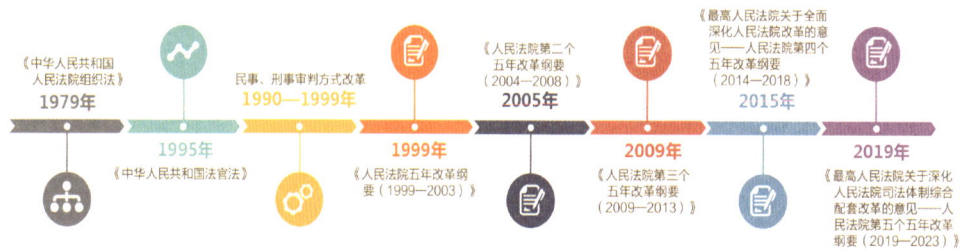

人民法院司法改革时间节点图

中国法院改革的组织实施

2014年初，中国成立以习近平总书记为组长的中央全面深化改革领导小组，负责改革的总体设计、统筹协调、整体推进、督促落实。2018年3月后，更名为中央全面深化改革委员会。2014年1月22日至2018年12月31日，中央全面深化改革领导小组、中央全面深化改革委员会共召开45次会议，审议通过涉及人民法院的重要改革文件35个。

中央全面深化改革委员会下设6个专项小组，负责研究相关领域重要改革问题，协调推动有关专项改革政策措施的制定和实施。深化司法体制改革工作由社会体制改革专项小组（中央司法体制改革领导小组）负责。

司法体制改革涉及面广、政策性强，考虑到完善司法人员分类管理、完善司法责任制、健全司法人员职业保障、推动省级以下地方法院人财物统一管理是司法体制改革的基础性措施，根据重大改革事项先行试点的原则，中国分三个批次，就上述四项措施在各省、自治区、直辖市进行试点，为全面推进改革积累经验。自 2014 年 6 月开始，上海、吉林、湖北、广东、海南、贵州、青海 7 个省、直辖市开展第一批司法体制改革试点；2015 年 6 月开始，山西、内蒙古、黑龙江、江苏、浙江、安徽、福建、山东、重庆、云南、宁夏 11 个省、自治区、直辖市开展第二批司法体制改革试点。2016 年 3 月，北京等其他 13 个省、自治区、直辖市及新疆维吾尔自治区生产建设兵团开展第三批司法体制改革试点。2016 年 7 月以后，上述四项重大改革在全国范围内全面推开。

中央全面深化改革委员会历次会议通过的司法改革文件一览图

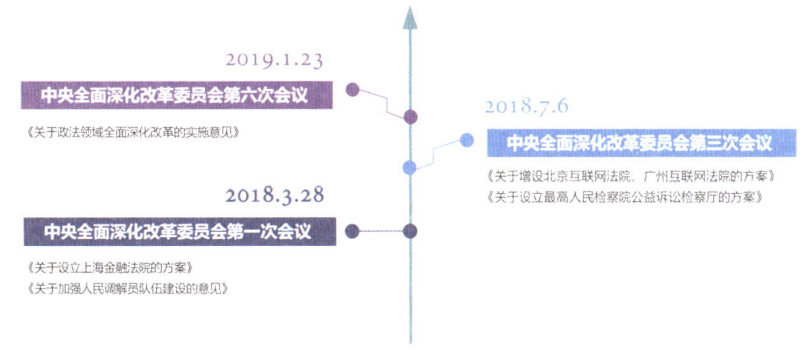

— 5 —

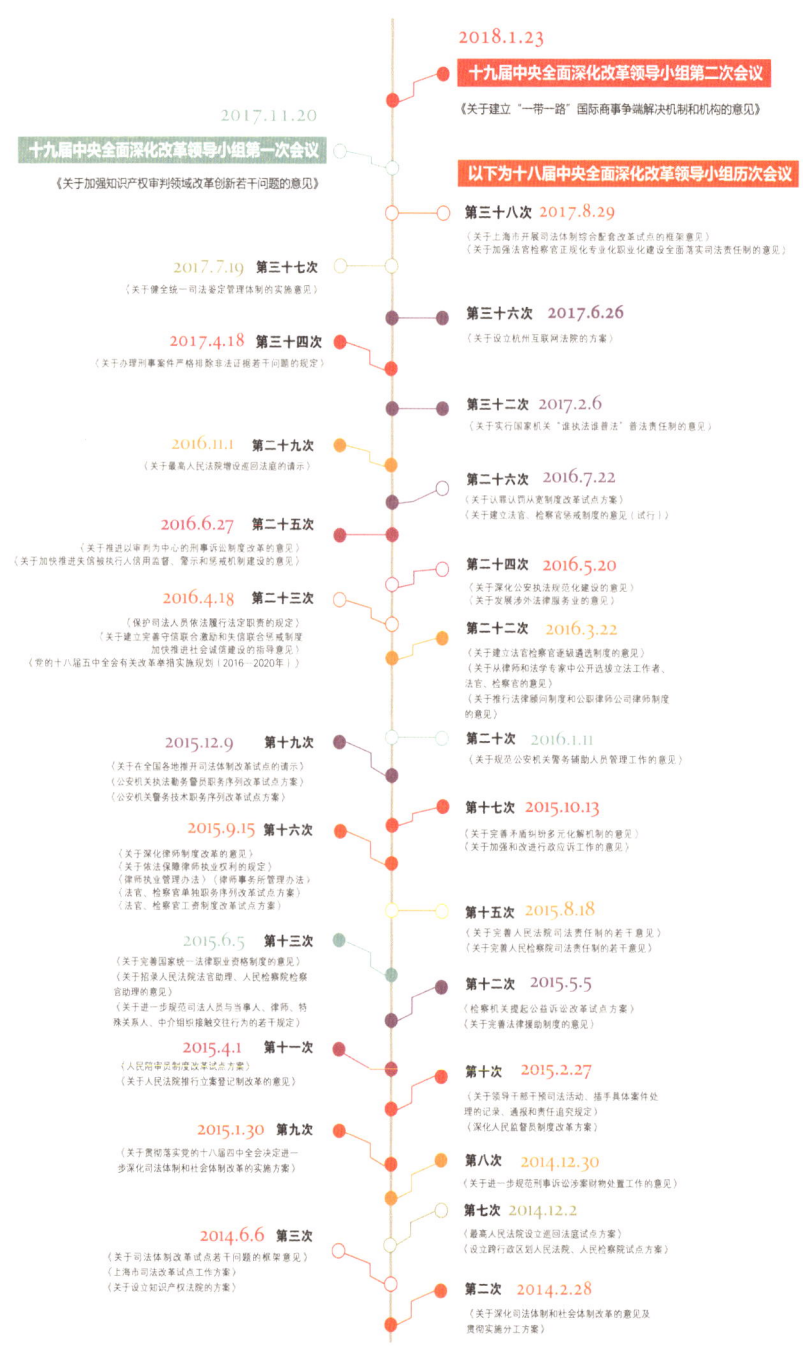

中央全面深化改革领导小组、中央全面深化改革委员会历次会议通过的
司法改革文件示意图

最高人民法院成立由首席大法官周强担任组长的司法改革领导小组，组织领导、统筹协调法院司法改革工作，召开全体会议和专题会议，统筹规划改革要点、研究审议改革方案、讨论决定重大问题。各高级人民法院分别成立司法改革领导小组，监督指导、统筹协调辖区内法院的司法改革工作。各高级人民法院拟就司法改革项目开展试点的，试点方案须报最高人民法院审批同意，重大改革试点方案须经最高人民法院报中央审批同意方可实施。

二、全面落实司法责任制

让审理者裁判、由裁判者负责，是司法规律的客观要求，也是深化司法体制改革的核心内容。2015年9月，最高人民法院印发关于完善人民法院司法责任制的若干意见，确定了新型审判权力运行机制，指导全国法院推进司法责任制改革。2018年12月，最高人民法院印发关于进一步全面落实司法责任制的实施意见，就完善审判监督管理机制、健全法律统一适用机制等问题加强指导，推动全面落实司法责任制。全面实行司法责任制改革后，全国法院一线审判力量增加20%以上，人均办案数量增长20%以上，结案率上升18%以上。

——实行独任法官、合议庭办案责任制。各级人民法院充分尊重独任法官、合议庭的法定审判组织地位，普遍建立"谁审理，谁裁判，谁负责"的办案责任制，基本取消案件层层请示、逐级审批。合议庭或者法官独任审理案件形成的裁判文书，经合议庭组成人员或者独任法官签署即印发。除审判委员会讨论决定的案件以外，院长、庭长不再审核签发自己未直接参加审理案件的裁判文书。改革后，全国法院由独任法官、合议庭直接作出裁判的案件达到案件总数的98%以上，提交审判委员会讨论的案件数量大幅下降。上海法院直接由独任法官、合议庭裁判的案件比例达99.9%，提交审判委员会讨论的案件仅占结案总数的0.1%。

——灵活组建审判团队。各基层人民法院根据法律规定和工作实际，统筹考虑繁简分流和审判专业化分工，组建以法官为核心、以法官助理、书记员等审判辅助人员为支撑的审判团队，制定法官、法官助理、书记员岗位职责清单，健全权责明晰、权责一致、分工协作、运转有序的办案工作机制，有效提升审判质量效率。北京市朝阳区人民法院按照繁简分流的思路，组建 26 个速裁团队，开展"简案快审"，每个团队年结案超过 650 件。组建 45 个专业审判团队，针对金融、知识产权、不动产、破产等专业审判领域，实行"繁案精审"，公正审理了一大批重大疑难复杂案件。广东省深圳市福田区人民法院优化审判团队组建模式。在速裁快审快执团队中，为每名法官配备多名助理；在普通审判团队中,由 1 名法官和 2 名助理组成相对固定基础办案单元，由 3 个办案单元组成一个审判团队，兼顾了审判团队的稳定性和灵活性,实现审判资源优化配置。2018 年,该院各类审判团队结案 107301 件，同比增长 16.32%，审判质效有效提升。

新型审判团队模式

审判团队组建模式示意图

——改革案件分配机制。各级人民法院建立"随机分案为主、指定分案为辅"的案件分配机制。根据审判领域类别和繁简分流安排，随机确定案件承办法官。对于存在回避情形，或者因工作调动、身体健康、廉政风险等事由确需调整承办法官的，由院长、庭长按权限审批决定，调整结果及时通知当事人，并在办案平台公开。上海法院制定关于实行随机自动分案的指导意见，实现全部民商事案件的随机分案。海南省三亚市城郊人民法院科学预设法官饱和工作量，引入自动分案系统，按照法官办案指标和未结案数，自动计算工作量后进行随机分案，以信息化手段解决案件分配不均问题。

——创新审判辅助工作模式。各级人民法院建立专门实施文书送达、财产保全、执行查控、文书上网、网络公告等事务的工作团队，对审判辅助事务实行集约化管理，提升工作效能。北京、上海、江苏、福建、广东等地法院积极探索以社会化购买服务形式处理通知送达、材料扫描、卷宗归档等辅助事务，借助外力提升办案效率。广东省深圳市中级人民法院制定法院购买社会化服务指导文件，明确法院购买社会化服务的范围、程序和标准，明确涉及诉讼服务、审判执行、法院管理、后勤保障、司法公开、信息化建设和文化建设等领域的七大类41项服务，可以向社会购买。2018年通过购买调解协助服务，该院已成功在诉前调解纠纷15829件，利用社会力量对20余万案件的纸质材料集中扫描、生成电子卷宗，办案效率不断提升。福建省厦门市思明区人民法院和厦门鹭江公证处创建全国首个诉讼与公证协同创新中心，明确公证机构可以协助人民法院开展程序性、辅助性司法辅助业务。

——健全院长庭长办案常态化机制。全国法院实行法官员额制，按照法官入额必须办案的要求，各级人民法院院长、庭长（含副职）入额后普遍回归审判一线。2017年4月，最高人民法院发布关于加强各级人民法院院长、庭长办理案件工作的指导意见，建立院长、庭长办案刚性约束和考核监督机制，健全院领导主要审理重大疑难复杂案件机制，充分发挥院长、庭长办案示范引领作用。2018 年，江苏法院院长、庭长担任承办法官或审判长审理案件占全省法院审理案件总数的 50.84%。

——健全新型审判监督管理机制。2017 年 4 月，最高人民法院印发关于落实司法责任制完善审判监督管理机制的意见，指导各地健全新型监督管理体系。各级人民法院制定院庭长权力职责清单和有关规定，规范院长、庭长行使审判监督管理权的范围和方式，积极运用信息化手段，构建全院全员全过程的监督管理机制。院长、庭长对案件的意见均通过专业法官会议、审判委员会公开提出，在办案平台上全程留痕，实现放权不放任、用权受监督。江苏、浙江、上海、四川等地法院，依托人工智能和大数据手段，探索运用自动化识别、标签化处理、系统推送、节点控制、权限冻结等方式实现监督智能化。天津市高级人民法院印发四批 29 类司法标准，涵盖审判流程、权力运行、司法公开、诉讼服务等方面。四川省成都市中级人民法院紧扣立案、审理、结案、上诉、执行五大环节，依托信息化办案平台，对 183 个工作节点、68 个监控节点实行全程静默化监督，辅助法官办理案件。

——健全主审法官会议制度。各级人民法院普遍建立主审法官会议制度，为法官正确适用法律提供咨询意见，讨论意见供合议庭参考。2018 年 12 月，最高人民法院发布关于健全完善人民法院主审法官会议工作机制的指导意见，完善专业法官会议议事规则。重庆市第二中级人民法院建立庭室内的法官联席会议和跨业务部门的法官会议制度，审判委员会研究案件同比减少 42%，发挥了法官会议服务咨询功能和过滤提交审判委员会讨论案件功能。

——改革审判委员会制度。最高人民法院制定指导意见，强化审判委员会总结审判经验、统一法律适用、讨论决定审判工作重大事项的职能。除法律规定不公开的外，审判委员会讨论案件的决定及其理由统一在裁判文书中公开。中级以上人民法院根据审判工作需要，按照审判委员会委员专业和工作分工，召开刑事审判、民事行政审判等专业委员会会议。除法律规定的情形和涉及国家外交、安全和社会稳定的重大复杂案件外，审判委员会主要讨论重大、疑难、复杂案件的法律适用问题。各级人民法院审判委员会讨论案件数量普遍较改革前显著下降。内蒙古自治区高级人民法院推进审判委员会制度改革后，审判委员会召开次数同比下降14.3%，讨论具体案件同比下降45.1%，审判委员会职能更聚焦于总结审判经验，讨论决定审判工作重大事项。海南全省法院推进审判委员会制度改革以来，审判委员会讨论案件数同比减少41.75%。

——建立案例指导和类案检索报告等制度。最高人民法院建立案例指导制度，制定案例指导工作实施细则，截至2018年底，共发布20批106件指导性案例。各级人民法院审理的案件，在基本案情和法律适用方面，与最高人民法院发布的指导性案例相类似的，应当参照相关指导性案例的裁判要点作出裁判，并将指导性案例作为裁判理由引述。各地普遍建立类案参考、裁判指引等制度。海南省高级人民法院建立类案参考信息库，有效减少“类案不同判”现象。湖南法院要求承办法官对存在法律适用争议或者“类案不同判”可能的案件，制作关联案件和检索报告。

——完善违法审判责任追究机制。最高人民法院印发规定，明确法官应当对其履行审判职责的行为承担责任，在职责范围内对办案质量终身负责，法官在审判活动中故意违法，或者因重大过失导致裁判错误并造成严重后果的，应当承担违法审判责任。明确了审判责任豁免的情形及条件。按照有权必有责、失职必担责的精神，明确院长、庭长因故意或者重大过失，不当行使审判监督权和审判管理权应当承担的监督管理责任。完善错案认定、调查、审议、追究程序，严格依法追究法官违法审判责任。

——建立法官惩戒制度。2016 年 10 月，最高人民法院印发关于建立法官惩戒制度的意见，建立由人民法院和法官惩戒委员会分工负责的法官惩戒制度。全国 27 个省（自治区、直辖市）在省一级设立由三级法院法官代表和社会有关人员参与的法官惩戒委员会，负责审议法官是否有违反审判职责的行为、是否存在故意或者重大过失、是否应当承担违法审判责任，并提出惩戒意见，实现依法及时惩戒与强化职业保障相统一。

——完善法官业绩考核制度。最高人民法院就完善法官业绩考核制度和分配绩效奖金印发指导意见，要求绩效考核奖金的发放，不与法官等级挂钩，主要依据责任轻重、办案质量、办案数量和办案难度等因素，向一线办案人员倾斜。各级人民法院坚持客观量化和主观评价相结合，以量化考核为主，充分考虑地域、审级、专业、部门之间的差异，因地制宜制定简便易行的法官业绩考核制度。

——建立领导干部、司法机关内部人员干预司法活动、过问具体案件的记录、通报和责任追究制度。中共中央办公厅、国务院办公厅印发领导干部干预司法活动、插手具体案件处理的记录、通报和责任追究规定，最高人民法院分别制定领导干部、司法机关内部人员干预过问案件的记录和责任追究实施办法。各级人民法院在案件信息管理系统中设立内、外部人员过问案件信息专库。对各类人员在诉讼程序之外递转的涉及具体案件的函文、信件或者口头意见，人民法院工作人员均应全面、如实、及时地予以记录。人民法院每季度对外部人员过问案件信息专库中涉及领导干部过问的内容进行汇总分析，列出特别报告事项，报送有关部门和上一级人民法院。人民法院工作人员不记录或者不如实记录的，以及主管领导授意不记录或者不如实记录的，将视情给予相应纪律处分。制度建立后，干预过问案件的情形显著减少，人民法院依法独立公正行使审判权制度保障更加牢固。

——**完善司法人员依法履职保障机制**。2017 年 2 月，最高人民法院印发保护法官依法履行法定职责的实施办法，明确法官依法办理案件不受行政机关、社会团体和个人的干涉；任何单位或者个人不得要求法官从事超出法定职责范围的事务；非因法定事由、非经法定程序，不得将法官调离、免职、辞退或者作出降级、撤职等处分；对干扰阻碍司法活动，威胁滋扰、报复陷害、侮辱诽谤、暴力伤害司法人员及其近亲属的行为，依法迅速从严惩处；对采取不实举报、诬告陷害、利用信息网络等方式侮辱诽谤法官的，依法追究法律责任，为法官依法履职创造良好制度环境。

三、推进法院组织机构改革

健全完善优化、协同、高效的法院组织体系和机构职能体系，是人民法院司法改革的重要内容和目标，是审判体系和审判能力现代化的重要支撑。2013 年以来，中国法院积极推进法院组织体系和内设机构改革，优化司法管辖和职权配置，促进专业化审判和扁平化管理相结合，为服务大局、司法为民、公正司法奠定坚实基础。

——**设立最高人民法院巡回法庭**。2015 年 1 月底，最高人民法院在深圳、沈阳分别设立第一巡回法庭、第二巡回法庭；2016 年 12 月底，在南京、郑州、重庆、西安分别设立第三、第四、第五、第六巡回法庭。最高人民法院巡回法庭是最高人民法院派驻地方的常设审判机构，审理最高人民法院依法确定的案件，巡回法庭的判决和裁定即最高人民法院的判决和裁定。自巡回法庭成立以来，截至 2018 年底，六个巡回法庭共审结案件 33335 件，占最高人民法院结案总数的 50.35%，就地化解涉诉信访纠纷，累计接待群众来访 117090 人次。各巡回法庭大力开展巡回审判，积极创新工作机制，有效实现审判重心下移，方便群众诉讼、工作效能提升，有力促进了社会和谐稳定，服务保障各巡回区法治建设，被人民群众亲切称为"家门口的最高人民法院"，为完善中国特色社会主义司法制度、推进全面依法治国发挥了重要作用。

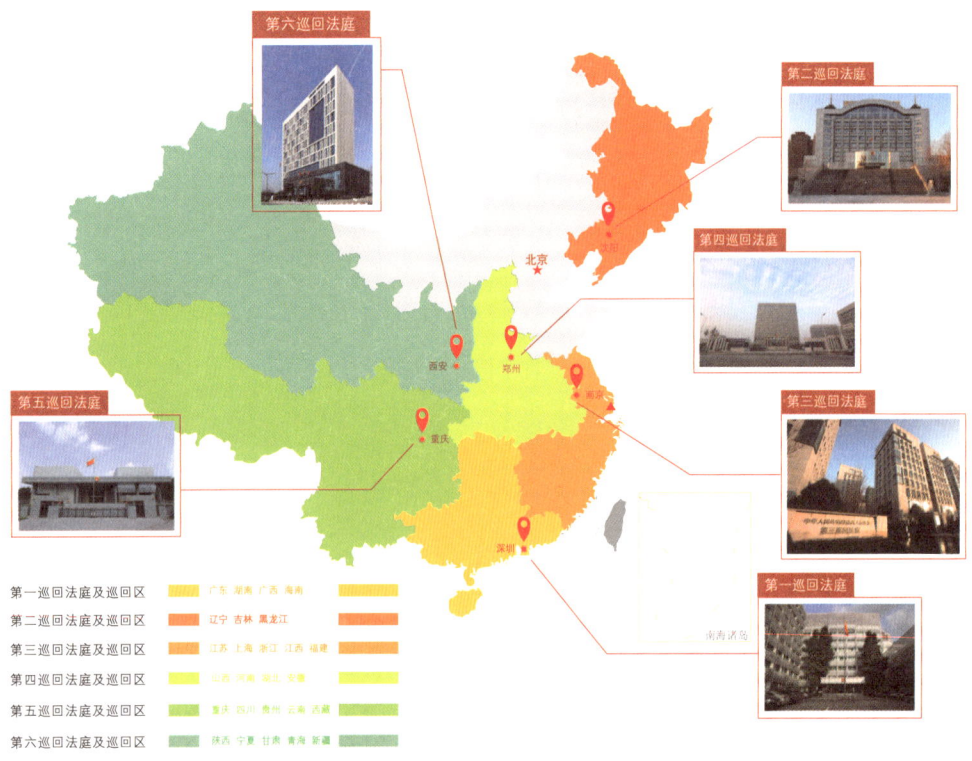

第六巡回法庭
第二巡回法庭
第四巡回法庭
第五巡回法庭
北京
西安 郑州
第三巡回法庭
重庆
深圳
第一巡回法庭
南海诸岛

第一巡回法庭及巡回区　　广东 湖南 广西 海南
第二巡回法庭及巡回区　　辽宁 吉林 黑龙江
第三巡回法庭及巡回区　　江苏 上海 浙江 江西 福建
第四巡回法庭及巡回区　　河南 山西 湖北 安徽
第五巡回法庭及巡回区　　重庆 四川 贵州 云南 西藏
第六巡回法庭及巡回区　　陕西 宁夏 甘肃 青海 新疆

最高人民法院巡回法庭分布图

　　——加强知识产权审判体系专门化建设。为进一步强化知识产权司法保护，统一知识产权案件裁判标准，根据全国人民代表大会常务委员会的决定，2014 年 11 月 6 日、12 月 16 日、12 月 28 日，北京、广州、上海知识产权法院相继成立。最高人民法院印发司法解释，确定知识产权法院案件管辖范围，并就知识产权法院法官选任工作、知识产权法院技术调查官参与诉讼活动等提出规范意见。知识产权法院通过公正审理典型案件、及时发布典型案例等方式，树立了中国知识产权司法保护的新形象。截至 2018 年底，三个知识产权法院共受理案件 90578 件，审结 74007 件。此外，最高人民法院还推动在江苏等 16个省市设立 19 个知识产权法庭，跨区域集中管辖部分知识产权案件。2019 年 1 月 1 日，根据全国人民代表大会常务委员会决定设立的最高人民法院知识产权法庭正式挂牌，统一审理专利等专业技术性较强的民事、行政上诉案件，建立形成国家层面知识产权案件上诉审理机制。上述改革举措，有效促进了知识产权案件审理专门化、管辖集中化、程序集约化，完善了中国特色知识产权审判体系。

——在北京、上海开展跨行政区划法院改革试点。为保障跨行政区划案件依法公正审判，2014年12月，在北京、上海分别设立北京市第四中级人民法院、上海市第三中级人民法院，作为跨行政区划人民法院试点，为探索建立普通案件在行政区划法院审理、特殊案件在跨行政区划法院审理的新型诉讼格局积累了经验。两个法院负责审理跨地区的重大民商事案件、重大行政案件、重大环境资源保护案件、重大食品药品安全案件和部分重大刑事案件，确保涉及地方利益的案件得到公正处理。2015年至2018年，北京市第四中级人民法院集中管辖以区县政府为被告的行政一审案件的收案量增幅高达650%。经最高人民法院指定，自2017年10月26日起，该院开始受理天津相关法院审理的环境保护行政案件上诉案件，迈出跨省级行政区划管辖案件的重要一步。上海市第三中级人民法院行政案件收案量每年增长30%以上，2018年行政案件和解撤诉数量同比增长126.67%。两个跨行政区划法院公正审理一系列具有重大社会影响的案件，有效破除了"诉讼主客场"现象，提升了司法公信力。

——设立上海金融法院。根据全国人民代表大会常务委员会的决定，2018年8月20日，上海金融法院正式挂牌设立，专门管辖应当由中级人民法院管辖的金融民商事案件和涉金融行政案件。最高人民法院印发司法解释，明确了上海金融法院具体管辖范围。截至2018年底，上海金融法院共收案1897件，标的总额达252亿元，案件主要类型涵盖证券虚假陈述责任纠纷、金融借款合同纠纷、公司债券交易纠纷、质押式证券回购纠纷、融资租赁合同纠纷、营业信托纠纷等。

——设立杭州、北京、广州互联网法院。互联网法院是中国法院主动适应互联网时代司法需求，贯彻落实网络强国战略的重大制度创新。2017 年 8 月 18 日、2018 年 9 月 9 日、9 月 28 日，杭州互联网法院、北京互联网法院、广州互联网法院相继挂牌设立。2018 年 9 月，最高人民法院印发关于互联网法院审理案件的司法解释，明确互联网法院的管辖范围、上诉机制、在线诉讼规则和诉讼平台建设要求。互联网法院积极推进"网上纠纷网上审理"，推动实现诉讼主体身份线上核实、证据材料在线提取、诉讼文书在线送达等，司法效率明显提升。杭州互联网法院在线立案率达到 89.2%，在线开庭率达到 59.9%，线上结案率达到 83.6%，在线庭审平均用时 28 分钟、平均审理期限 41 天，比传统审理模式分别节约时间 60% 和 50%。互联网法院注重总结提炼涉网案件裁判规则，公正高效审理了一批新类型、疑难复杂互联网案件，包括大数据权利归属、网络购物缔约过失责任、人工智能作品著作权权属等案件，有力推动了网络空间治理法治化。

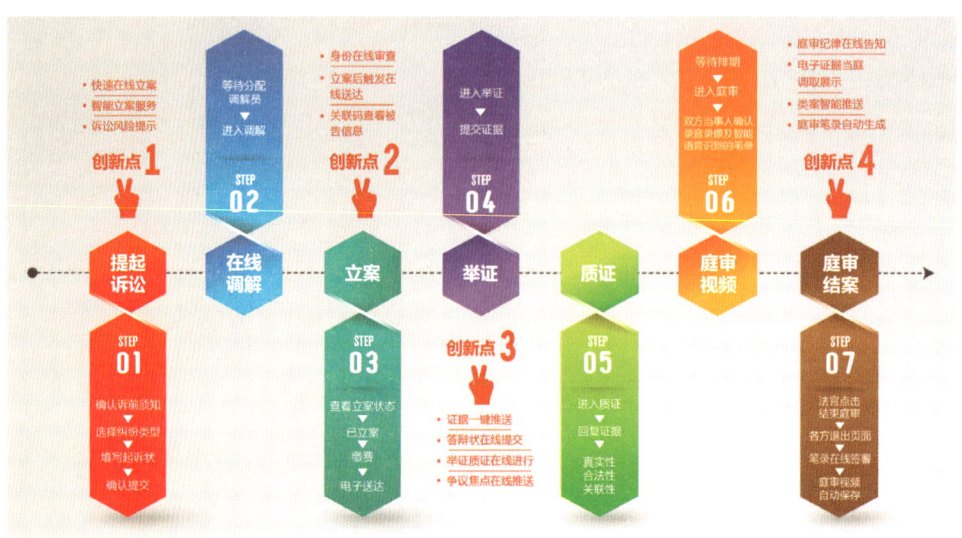

互联网法院在线审理机制示意图

——**改革军事法院组织体系**。军事法院是国家设立在军队的审判机关。根据中央统一部署，军事法院由过去按照军兵种和系统设置的模式改革为主要按照战区设置。改革后，新的军事法院组织体系包括：中国人民解放军军事法院（高级法院层级）；中国人民解放军东部战区军事法院、南部战区军事法院、西部战区第一、第二军事法院、北部战区军事法院、中部战区军事法院、总直属军事法院（中级法院层级）；中国人民解放军上海军事法院、南京军事法院、杭州军事法院等 26 个军事法院（基层法院层级）。

——**推进省以下人民法院内设机构改革**。最高人民法院会同中央有关部门，积极推进省以下人民法院内设机构改革。按照协同优化高效的原则，精简设置人民法院内设机构，严格控制内设机构数量，科学设置审判业务部门，整合职能交叉、业务相近的非审判业务机构，推进扁平化管理。截至 2018 年底，天津、上海已经完成内设机构改革任务，天津市中级、基层人民法院的内设机构数量由改革前的 361 个减少至 234 个，减幅达 35.2%；上海市 17 家基层人民法院内设机构（不含人民法庭）从 298 个精简至 197 个，减幅达 33.9%。其他省（区、市）基层法院内设机构改革也已进入方案审批备案程序。

四、强化人权司法保障制度机制

尊重和保障人权，是《中华人民共和国宪法》确立的重要原则，也是中国特色社会主义司法制度的重要内容。中国法院通过推进以审判为中心的刑事诉讼制度改革，严格落实罪刑法定、证据裁判、疑罪从无等法律原则，切实防止冤假错案，依法保障律师执业权利，在人权司法保障机制建设上取得积极成果。

——推进以审判为中心的刑事诉讼制度改革。最高人民法院会同最高人民检察院、公安部、国家安全部、司法部印发关于推进以审判为中心的刑事诉讼制度改革的指导意见和关于办理刑事案件严格排除非法证据的文件。以审判为中心的刑事诉讼制度改革贯彻证据裁判、非法证据排除、疑罪从无等原则，大力推进庭审实质化，完善审判对侦查、起诉活动的监督制约机制，从源头上防范刑讯逼供、非法取证等违法行为，推动形成诉讼以审判为中心、审判以庭审为中心、庭审以证据为中心的刑事诉讼格局，确保侦查、起诉、审判的案件事实经得起法律检验。2017 年 6 月，最高人民法院在全国 18 个中级人民法院开展办理刑事案件庭前会议、排除非法证据、第一审普通程序法庭调查规程试点，并自 2018 年 1 月 1 日起在全国法院试行。各地全面落实证据裁判原则，扎实推进庭审实质化，完善关键证人、鉴定人、侦查人员出庭作证制度，最大限度地发挥证人、鉴定人、侦查人员出庭的功能作用，有效解决控辩双方争议。广东法院 2017 年受理申请排除非法证据案件 1582 件，启动排除非法证据程序 1424 件，排除非法证据

235 件，超过前三年总和。四川省成都市中级人民法院在全国率先开展庭审实质化改革，通过全面落实庭前会议、严格排除非法证据、关键人证出庭、当庭认证、当庭宣判、律师辩护全覆盖、裁判文书繁简分流、召开示范庭等，保证庭审在查明事实、认定证据、保护诉权、公正裁判中发挥决定性作用。试点示范案件共有 1469 名人证出庭，其中一般证人 818 人，鉴定人 114 人，侦查人员 455 人，有专门知识的人 17 人，被害人 65 人。浙江省温州市中级人民法院完善出庭作证人员保护机制，印发侦查人员出庭作证的实施细则，设置远程作证室、证人面部遮蔽装置等设施，会同公安、检察机关探索建立证人权益保护联动机制，制定证人出庭费用补助标准。2015 年以来，全市法院共在 915 件刑事案件中通知 1434 人出庭，实际有 581 件案件 915 人出庭作证，出庭作证率为 63.8%。

——预防和纠正冤假错案。最高人民法院就健全防范刑事冤假错案工作机制提出指导意见，要求对于定罪证据不足的案件，应当依法宣告被告人无罪，不得降格或者变通作出"留有余地"的判决。2016 年 12 月 2 日，最高人民法院第二巡回法庭对原审被告人聂树斌故意杀人、强奸妇女再审案公开宣判，宣告撤销原审判决，改判聂树斌无罪。这起历时 22 年的重大疑难复杂案件得以纠正，彰显了对人权司法保障的高度重视和对证据裁判、疑罪从无等法律原则的坚定实践。2013 年以来，人民法院通过审判监督程序纠正聂树斌案、呼格吉勒图案、张氏叔侄案等重大刑事冤假错案 46 起，涉及 94 人，提振了全社会对司法公正的信心。2014 年至 2018 年，各级人民法院共依法宣告 4868 名被告人无罪，依法保障无罪者不受追究。

——完善刑事速裁程序和认罪认罚从宽制度。根据全国人民代表大会常务委员会的授权，2014 年 8 月 26 日开始，中国在北京等 18 个城市 217 个基层法院开展为期两年的刑事案件速裁程序改革试点。试点期间，试点法院适用速裁程序审结刑事案件 52540 件 54572 人，占试点法院同期判处一年以下有期徒刑以下刑罚案件的 35.88%，占同期全部刑事案件的 18.48%，10 日内审结的占 92.35%，比简易程序高 65.04 个百分点，当庭宣判率达 96.05%，比简易程序高 41.22 个百分点。北京市海淀区人民法院探索全流程速裁模式，有效压缩案件流转各环节在途时间，被告人在押案件诉讼全程平均用时 33 天，比改革前适用简易程序审结的同类案件用时减少约 70%。全部速裁案件中，附带民事诉讼原告人上诉率为 0，被告人上诉率为 2.01%，检察机关抗诉率仅为 0.01%，上诉抗诉率比全部刑事案件低 9.52 个百分点。中国政法大学开展的第三方评估显示，被告人对速裁程序运行效果满意度达 97.69%。速裁程序通过减少审前羁押，对被告人从快处理、从宽量刑，更好发挥社区矫正功能，促使罪犯改造和回归社会。2016 年 9 月，十二届全国人大常委会第二十二次会议审议了试点情况报告，充分肯定了试点工作，决定将刑事速裁试点改革统一纳入认罪认罚从宽制度改革继续试点。2016 年 9 月至 2018 年 9 月，共确定试点法院 281 个，适用认罪认罚从宽制度审结刑事案件 205510 件，占试点法院同期审结刑事案件的 53.5%。2018 年 10 月 26 日，十三届全国人大常委会第六次会议通过关于修改《中华人民共和国刑事诉讼法》的决定，将认罪认罚从宽制度改革试点成果吸收到新修订的刑事诉讼法中并在全国推行。

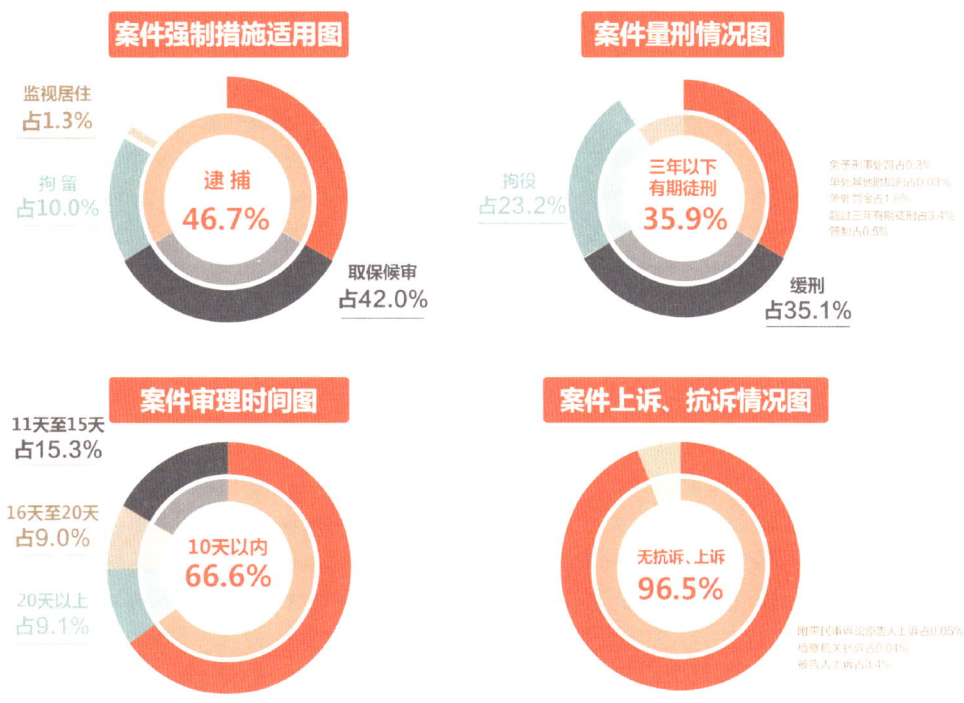

刑事案件认罪认罚从宽制度改革成效示意图

——深化量刑规范化改革。2013 年底，最高人民法院印发人民法院量刑指导意见，规范法官量刑裁量权，设置独立的量刑辩论程序，在全国范围内推进量刑规范化工作。2016 年，最高人民法院进一步扩大量刑规范化罪名和刑种试点，将危险驾驶等八种罪名纳入规范范围，从有期徒刑、拘役扩大到罚金、缓刑，指定部分法院开展试点工作，确保规范量刑、罪刑相适、罚当其罪。量刑规范化改革以来，量刑方法更加规范、科学，量刑结果更加公正、均衡，量刑程序更加公开、公正。

——严格规范减刑、假释和暂予监外执行。2014 年 4 月，最高人民法院印发关于减刑、假释案件审理程序的司法解释，建立减刑、假释公开审理制度和典型案例定期公布制度。2015 年开通全国法院减刑、假释、暂予监外执行信息网，向社会公众公开减刑假释案件从立案到

文书的全流程信息，让减刑假释司法活动全程在阳光下运行。2016 年
11 月，最高人民法院发布关于办理减刑、假释案件具体应用法律的规定，
进一步明确减刑、假释的性质、适用要求，统一全国减刑、假释案件
裁判标准，促进减刑、假释案件办理的公平公正。2017 年 11 月，最高
人民法院开通全国减刑假释信息化办案平台，实现人民法院与检察机
关、刑罚执行机关以及上下级人民法院之间案件信息互通、网上协同
办案，确保减刑假释案件审理全程留痕、全程监督。

——修改完善人民法院法庭规则。2015 年 2 月，最高人民法院、
公安部印发通知，规定人民法院开庭时，刑事被告人或上诉人不再穿
着看守所的识别服出庭受审，正在服刑的罪犯不再穿着监狱的囚服出
庭受审。人民法院提解在押刑事被告人或上诉人的，看守所应当将穿
着正装或便装的在押刑事被告人或上诉人移交人民法院，彰显了现代
司法文明。2016 年 4 月 13 日，最高人民法院印发新修订的《中华人民
共和国人民法院法庭规则》，进一步明确法庭行为规范、维护法庭秩序，
强化人权司法保障，促进法庭更加开放、便民、文明、安全，让法庭
成为人民群众感知公平正义的场所。

——完善保障律师依法履职制度。2015 年 12 月，最高人民法院印
发关于依法保障律师诉讼权利的意见，依法保障律师知情权、阅卷权、
出庭权、辩论辩护权、申请调取证据权、申请排除非法证据权、代理
申诉权等执业权利，为律师依法履职提供保障和便利。建立死刑复核
案件听取律师意见制度，保障律师查询立案信息、查阅案卷材料等权
利，律师可直接向最高人民法院法官当面陈述辩护意见，确保死刑复
核案件质量。2017 年 10 月，最高人民法院、司法部印发关于开展刑事
案件律师辩护全覆盖试点工作的办法，在上海、浙江等地开展刑事案
件审判阶段律师辩护全覆盖试点工作。2015 年 12 月 30 日，最高人民

法院开通律师服务平台，实现网上立案、网上阅卷、联系法官等功能。截至 2018 年底，全国 1924 家法院开通律师服务平台，共为律师提供服务 127 万次。最高人民法院的律师服务平台已为 22067 家律师事务所，89338 名律师提供网上立案、网上阅卷、案件查询、网上缴费、网上退费、电子送达、联系法官等服务。2018 年律师服务平台访问量 43527 人次，与去年相比，增加 3 倍以上。浙江三级法院设立律师服务中心，提供案件信息查询、卷宗查阅、会见法官、休息更衣等服务，探索在律师事务所开设网上办理诉讼事项专用设施。

——完善国家赔偿制度。最高人民法院制定关于办理刑事赔偿案件适用法律若干问题的解释，完善赔偿案件质证程序，规范精神损害抚慰金裁量标准，就进一步加强刑事冤错案件国家赔偿工作提出意见，充分发挥国家赔偿的权利救济功能。2014 年至 2018 年，各级人民法院受理国家赔偿案件 31434 件。呼格吉勒图案、张氏叔侄案、聂树斌案、刘忠林案等刑事冤错案件的受害人或其近亲属依法及时获得赔偿。其中，刘忠林收到赔偿义务机关吉林省辽源市中级人民法院国家赔偿金 460 万元。

——完善司法救助制度。2016 年 7 月，最高人民法院印发关于加强和规范人民法院国家司法救助工作的意见，统一案件受理、救助范围、救助程序、救助标准、经费保障、资金发放，实现救助制度法治化、救助案件司法化。2016 年 9 月 18 日，最高人民法院设立司法救助委员会，地方各级人民法院也相继成立司法救助委员会。天津法院在司法救助工作中，加强与其他司法机关、社会救助和外省市救助的联动，实现司法救助与社会保障的无缝对接，提高了救助的精准度、覆盖面和时效性。四川法院简化司法救助办理流程，开发运行司法救助网络运行平台，实现救助案件办理网络化、规范化。

——规范处理涉案财物的司法程序。2014 年 10 月，最高人民法院印发关于刑事裁判涉财产部分执行的司法解释，规范没收财产、追缴、变价措施、执行异议等刑事涉案财物执行程序。2015 年至 2018 年，最高人民法院会同中央有关部门，不断推动建立跨部门的地方涉案财物集中管理信息平台，完善涉案财物先行处置程序、审前返还程序，明确利害关系人诉讼权利，完善权利救济和责任追究机制。2015 年 5 月，浙江省诸暨市成立全国首家跨部门的刑事诉讼涉案财物管理中心，建立涉案财物管理统一信息平台，政法各部门各自管理的涉案财物信息统一进入平台，实现涉案财物电子化移送，方便了办案进程，规范了涉案财物处理程序。

五、完善司法便民利民制度机制

司法为民、公正司法是人民法院的工作主线。人民法院通过改革案件受理制度，加强诉讼服务中心和人民法庭建设，健全矛盾纠纷多元化解机制和案件繁简分流机制，推进家事审判方式改革等，不断提升司法为民水平，让人民群众在司法改革中有更多获得感。

——全面落实立案登记制改革。从 2015 年 5 月 1 日起，人民法院改革案件受理制度，变立案审查制为立案登记制，对符合受理条件的起诉，做到有案必立、有诉必理，切实保障当事人诉权，从制度上、源头上彻底解决了"立案难"问题。截至 2018 年底，全国法院登记立案数量超过 6489 万件，当场登记立案率超过 95%。各地法院普遍简化立案程序，采取立案告知书、一次性补正清单、限时答复等方式，努力保障当事人一次性成功立案。北京法院建立立案监督和投诉迅速处理工作机制，对当事人反映和投诉立案工作中存在的问题及时回应、依法纠正，仅 2016 年就接待和处理不立案投诉 1300 余人次，确保了立案登记制改革有效落实。最高人民法院加大改革督察力度，坚决制止另设条件限制立案的做法，防止立案难问题反弹回潮。

——构建多元化登记立案新模式。人民法院依托信息技术，推进多种便民立案方式，形成了以当场立案为主体，以网上立案、自助立案、跨域立案、协作立案等为支撑的立案新格局，人民群众诉讼更加方便快捷，立案效率显著提升。各地法院在积极畅通大厅立案、预约立案、上门立案等常规立案渠道的同时，大力推进网上立案，当事人足不出户即可完成立案手续。积极探索跨域立案服务，当事人可以就近或自愿选择任一法院作为协作法院，提交诉讼服务申请，完成立案手续，减轻了当事人异地立案的负担。截至2018年底，全国3044家法院开通网上立案服务，共网上立案238万件；1154家法院提供跨域立案服务，办理跨域立案12万件；1863家法院设立自助立案区，当事人或律师自助立案103万件。京津冀三地7家法院建立协作立案新模式，让当事人可以不受地域限制享受普惠均等、便捷高效的立案服务。上海市浦东新区人民法院开发二维码自助立案系统，每个案件平均立案时间只有15分钟。

立案登记制改革成效示意图

——加强诉讼服务现代化建设。2014 年 12 月，最高人民法院就全面推进人民法院诉讼服务中心建设提出指导意见。到 2018 年底，全国 98% 的法院建立了诉讼服务大厅，面积达 182 万平方米，2995 家法院开通了诉讼服务网，1623 家法院上线诉讼服务 APP，2813 家法院设立 12368 诉讼服务热线。各级法院大力建设 24 小时自助法院、在线调解室、电子阅卷室、视频接访室等网上办公场所，配备智能访客系统、导诉机器人、诉讼辅导机、诉讼风险评估机、便民服务自助终端、智能云柜、智能导航等设备，通过各类服务平台，实现网上立案、网上缴费、在线调解、查询信息、递交材料、网上阅卷、电子送达、联系法官等，诉讼服务功能达 48 项，比 2009 年时增加 40 项。在人民法院诉讼服务中心大力推进繁简分流，开展"分流＋调解＋速裁＋快审"机制改革，设立程序分流员，开辟专门调解场地，建设开放式速裁法庭，优化诉调对接机制，配足分流调解速裁快审人员力量，运行"分调裁审"信息系统，形成基层法院多数案件在诉讼服务中心通过调解、速裁、快审一站式解决，切实发挥诉讼服务中心门诊解纷功能。全国法院普遍开展"分调裁审"机制改革，2464 家法院设立了程序分流员，共有 14669 名分流员开展繁简分流工作，引入专职调解员 12234 人。截至 2018 年底，全国法院诉前多元化解案件 171 万件，立案后调解案件 120 万件，在诉讼服务中心通过速裁快审解决案件 175 万件。安徽法院在诉讼服务中心设立家事、劳动、物业纠纷等纠纷调解窗口，设立"两代表一委员"工作站、律师工作室及人民调解室，开展矛盾纠纷在线调解、远程调解、多元化解，取得了良好效果。浙江法院开展"最多跑一次"改革，通过拓展线上线下多种服务渠道，减轻群众诉累。西藏、宁夏等地法院使用车载流动法庭，为当事人提供便捷诉讼服务。

——健全多元化纠纷解决机制。多元化纠纷解决机制是国家治理体系现代化建设中的重要组成部分。2016年6月，最高人民法院印发关于人民法院进一步深化多元化纠纷解决机制改革的意见，提出"国家制定发展战略、司法发挥保障作用、推动国家立法进程"的"三步走战略"，确立"国家主导、司法推动、社会参与、多元并举、法治保障"的现代纠纷解决理念。最高人民法院分别与公安部、司法部、人社部、民政部、发改委、中国证监会、中国保监会、中国侨联、全国工商联、全国妇联等部门就人民调解、家事纠纷、证券期货纠纷、保险纠纷、公证参与法院司法辅助事务等领域联合发布20多个诉调对接文件，建立立体的多元纠纷解决体系。最高人民法院印发关于人民法院特邀调解的规定，指导各地加强诉调对接，促进矛盾纠纷及时高效化解。截至2018年底，全国法院设置诉调对接中心3320个，吸纳特邀调解组织近22194个，特邀调解员达78153人，接受法院委派、委托调解案件1862800件。各级人民法院建立形式多样、运行规范的诉调对接平台，发挥案件分流、先行调解、委派调解、委托调解、司法确认等制度功能，健全法院与行政机关、人民调解组织、行业调解组织、商事调解组织、仲裁机构、公证机构的衔接机制。创新"互联网＋纠纷解决"，建立统一在线调解平台，截至2018年12月底，1258家法院开展在线调解，化解纠纷11394件。北京法院2018年通过"多元调解＋速裁"导出一审民事案件30.4万件，多元调解成功和速裁结案17.6万件，占同期一审民事结案量的39%。浙江法院建设在线矛盾纠纷多元化解平台，形成递进式、漏斗型的矛盾纠纷分层过滤化解机制。截至2018年11月底，平台注册用户达43.2万人，注册调解员3.4万人，申请调解案件24万余件，调解成功20.8万件，调解成功率达88.17%，传承创新"枫桥经验"，推动从"小事不出村"升级到"解纷不出户"。安徽省马鞍山市中级人民法院打造多元改革升级版，开展异地远程网上调解等工作，网上调解成功率达 95.1%。四川省眉山市中级人民法院充分调动和运用各类纠纷解决资源，在 2014 年至 2016 年实现 80.72% 的矛盾纠纷通过非诉方式化解，真正进入审判程序通过裁判处理的案件仅占 7.06%，形成了诉非衔接的"眉山经验"。黑龙江省、安徽省、福建省、山东省及福建省厦门市印发了矛盾纠纷多元化解地方性法规，为纠纷解决和社会治理提供了法治保障。

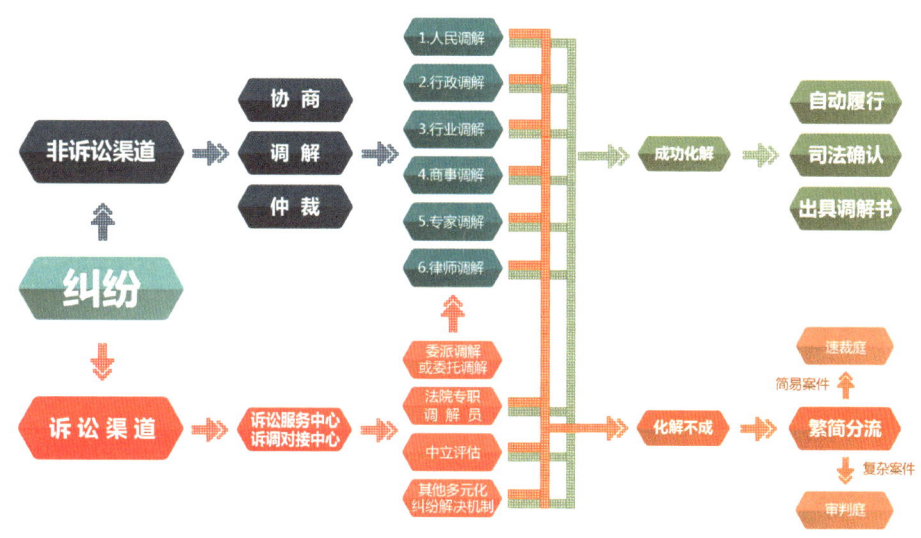

多元化纠纷解决机制示意图

——建立完善律师调解制度。2017 年 9 月，最高人民法院、司法部联合印发关于开展律师调解试点工作的意见，在北京、黑龙江、上海等 11 个省（直辖市）进行试点。试点工作开展一年多以来，试点法院共建立律师调解工作室 657 个，加入法院特邀调解名册的律师调解组织 1290 个、律师调解员 12360 名；律师参与调解案件 54898 件，调解成功 25569 件；申请司法确认 8529 件，发出支付令 824 件，对调解协议申请强制执行 3325 件，有效发挥律师群体在纠纷化解中的优势和作用。全国 63% 的法院建立律师代理申诉制度，78% 的法院建立律师驻点工作制度。截至 2018 年底，全国法院律师驻点接待案件 791932 件，代理申诉案件 26942 件，参与化解案件 27499 件。

——推进案件繁简分流机制改革。2016 年 9 月，最高人民法院印发关于进一步推进案件繁简分流优化司法资源配置的意见。2017 年 5 月，印发关于民商事案件繁简分流和调解速裁操作规程，指导各级人民法院优化司法资源配置，创新完善工作机制，缓解人案矛盾。最高人民法院制定案件繁简分流机制改革示范法院标准，确定 80 个示范法院，发挥示范带动作用。2018 年，适用简易程序审结案件较 2014 年上升 38.81%。各地积极开展要素式庭审、令状式文书、示范性诉讼等机制创新，以深化改革破解案件数量增长较快的新问题，缩短办案周期，提高司法效率。江苏全省大部分基层法院设立小额速裁组（庭），保证 1 名法官配备 1 名书记员，推行要素式裁判方式，简化制作裁判文书，原则上当庭宣判，平均审理天数不到 20 天，案件调解撤诉率接近 70%。辽宁省沈阳市中级人民法院积极推行庭前会议，将庭审中权利义务告知、回避申请等程序性工作前置，明确诉辩意见，固定无争议事实，归纳争议焦点并促使当事人围绕焦点举证，改革后庭审时间与以往相比平均缩短 50 分钟。

——深化涉诉信访制度改革。最高人民法院积极推动信访工作法治化，各级人民法院完善诉访分离工作机制，切实解决群众合法合理诉求。最高人民法院建设网上申诉信访平台，当事人只需填写申诉信访信息，提交相应材料，即可随时随地查询申诉信访办理进程和反馈结果，进一步畅通了申诉信访渠道，减少了人民群众奔波之苦。开通远程视频接访系统，贯通全国四级法院，实现最高人民法院、地方相关人民法院和信访人之间的多方远程面对面交流，涉诉进京访数量同比降低约 30%。最高人民法院初步建成全国法院涉诉信访平台，汇聚全国法院信访信息，实现信访信息发布、信息报送、信访监督等功能应用以及上下级法院涉诉信访信息的快速、准确沟通，提高了信访工作效率，完善了统一协调机制。

——推进家事审判方式和工作机制改革。2016 年 4 月，最高人民法院印发关于开展家事审判方式和工作机制改革试点工作的指导意见，探索家事纠纷的专业化、社会化和人性化解决方式，积极推进家事审判方式和工作机制改革试点。试点法院建立家事审判庭或者家事审判团队，引入家事调查员、社工陪护及儿童心理专家等，为当事人提供心理疏导等相关专业服务，推动整合司法、行政和社会多方力量，建设新型家事纠纷综合协调解决机制。2017 年 7 月 19 日，最高人民法院牵头建立包括 15 个单位共同参与的家事审判方式和工作机制改革联席会议制度。2018 年 7 月 18 日，最高人民法院印发关于进一步深化家事审判方式和工作机制改革的意见。河北、山东、浙江、福建、陕西、青海、甘肃、西藏等地法院纷纷建立多部门参与的联席会议制度，推动形成"党委领导、政府尽责、法院牵头、社会参与"的工作格局。辽宁、内蒙古、安徽、宁夏、广西等高级人民法院制定全面的家事案件审理规程。重庆、青海等地法院加强家事案件心理测评干预，有效防止"民转刑"案件发生；上海市普陀区人民法院创设"儿童权益代表人"机制，由妇儿工委办公室人员作为代表人，通过独立调查、取证、参与庭审，切实保护未成年人合法权益；山西省临汾市中级人民法院积极探索家事案件回访帮扶制度，让人民群众充分感受社会主义司法的温度。北京市西城区人民法院、湖北省宜昌市夷陵区人民法院积极适用婚姻冷静期制度。

——推进道路交通事故损害赔偿纠纷"网上数据一体化处理"改革试点。针对我国道路交通纠纷日渐增多、人民群众化解此类纠纷耗时费力的突出矛盾，最高人民法院首先在杭州市余杭区开展道路交通事故纠纷"网上数据一体化处理"综合改革试点。2017年11月，最高人民法院与公安部、司法部、中国保监会联合召开会议，决定在北京等14个省（自治区、直辖市）联合开展试点工作，在全国推行道交纠纷"网上数据一体化处理"工作，将公安交通管理部门的责任认定、相关主体的理赔计算、调解组织的调解、鉴定机构的鉴定、法院的诉讼、保险行业的理赔等纠纷处理流程全部实现在线处置，实现信息共享、工作联动，做到一网办案、一键理赔、快速处理，让纠纷解决更方便、更快捷。2017年、2018年，全国分别调解道路交通事故损害赔偿民事第一审纠纷近37万件和36万件，有的试点地区通过改革，诉至法院的道交纠纷下降了50%。

——改革完善民事送达制度。2017年7月，最高人民法院印发关于进一步加强民事送达工作的若干意见，全面推进当事人送达地址确认制度，统一送达地址确认书格式，规范送达地址确认书内容，积极探索电子送达及送达凭证保全的有效方式方法，提升民事送达质量效率，着力解决制约民事审判工作的瓶颈之一"送达难"。浙江省温岭市人民法院设立送达管理中心，配备9名专职送达人员，开发送达管理软件，开通送达管理中心官方微信，加强与邮政送达协调，初步实现送达全程信息化、集约化、规范化管理，提高了送达效率。四川省德阳市旌阳区人民法院综合运用电子送达、公证送达、约定送达、司法建议等多种方式，送达成本降低50%。实施电子送达后，涉保险合同类案件仅送达签收环节就可节约5天以上，整个案件审理周期节约10天以上。

——加强人民法庭建设。2014 年 12 月，最高人民法院印发关于进一步加强新形势下人民法庭工作的若干意见，指导各地加强人民法庭建设，切实落实司法为民宗旨。积极推进以中心法庭为主、社区法庭和巡回审判点为辅的法庭布局形式，优化人民法庭的区域布局和人员比例。河南法院建成法院信息中心，全省派出法庭全面实现网络互联互通与数据共联共享，开发电子签章系统和电子卷宗跨域流转功能，实现部分案件跨县市区异地立案，方便当事人就近选择法院或人民法庭办理立案事务。重庆法院大力加强法庭联系点建设，设立便民诉讼站，方便群众诉讼。

六、扎实推进"基本解决执行难"

生效法律文书的执行，是实现司法公正的"最后一公里"，事关司法权威和司法公信力的有效提升。2016 年 3 月，最高人民法院在第十二届全国人民代表大会第四次会议上提出"用两到三年时间基本解决执行难问题"。2016 年 4 月，最高人民法院印发《关于落实"用两到三年时间基本解决执行难问题"的工作纲要》，确定"基本解决执行难"的总体目标，为确保如期实现总体目标，最高人民法院进一步提出"四个 90%，一个 80%"的核心指标要求，作为阶段性目标，即 90% 以上有财产可供执行案件在法定期限内执结，90% 以上无财产可供执行案件终结本次执行程序符合规范要求，90% 以上执行信访案件得到化解或办结，全国 90% 以上法院达标，近三年执行案件整体执结率超过 80%。

"基本解决执行难"目标提出以来，人民法院全面推进执行信息化、规范化建设，不断深化执行体制机制和管理模式改革，持续加强队伍建设，加大投入保障力度，全面打响"基本解决执行难"攻坚战。2016 年至 2018 年底，全国法院共受理执行案件 2043.5378 万件，执结 1936.1165 万件，执行到位金额 4.4 万亿元，同比分别增长 98.45%、105.09% 和 71.2%。

——推动形成综合治理"执行难"工作格局。2016 年 6 月，中央深改组审议通过关于加快推进失信被执行人信用监督、警示和惩戒机制建设的意见。全国 31 个省（自治区、直辖市）全部印发支持人民法院解决执行难、加强失信被执行人信用惩戒的文件，12 个省（自治区、直辖市）人大常委会专门印发支持人民法院解决执行难的决定。目前，党委领导、政法委协调、人大监督、政府支持、法院主办、部门配合、社会参与的综合治理执行难工作格局已初步形成，并不断完善，为"基本解决执行难"奠定了坚实基础。

——推进网络查控系统建设。针对传统执行查控模式存在的执行效率低、覆盖财产范围窄、查控人力成本高等难题，最高人民法院建立"总对总"网络查控系统，与公安部、民政部、自然资源部、交通运输部、人民银行、中国银行保险监督管理委员会等 16 家单位和 3900 多家银行业金融机构联网，可以查询被执行人全国范围内的不动产、存款、金融理财产品、船舶、车辆、证券、网络资金等 16 类 25 项信息，基本实现对被执行人主要财产形式和相关信息的有效覆盖，极大提升了执行效率，实现了执行查控方式的根本变革。截至 2018 年底，全国法院通过网络查控系统，为 6038 万案件提供查询冻结服务，共冻结资金 4136 亿元，查询房屋、土地等不动产信息 984 万条，车辆 5142 万辆，证券 1421 亿股，船舶 193.9 万艘，网络资金 257.1 亿元，有力维护了胜诉当事人合法权益。

——完善失信被执行人联合惩戒制度机制。2013 年，最高人民法院建立失信被执行人名单制度，推动对失信被执行人进行联合惩戒，努力破解规避执行难题。2016 年以来，最高人民法院与国家发改委等 60 家单位签署文件，推进失信被执行人信用监督、警示和惩戒机制建设，采取 11 类 37 大项 150 项惩戒措施，对失信被执行人担任公职、党代表、人大代表、政协委员以及出行、购房、投资、招投标等进行限制。截至 2018 年底，全国法院累计发布失信被执行人名单 1288 万例，共限制 1746 万人次购买机票，限制 547 万人次购买动车、高铁票，351 万名失信被执行人迫于信用惩戒压力自动履行了义务。

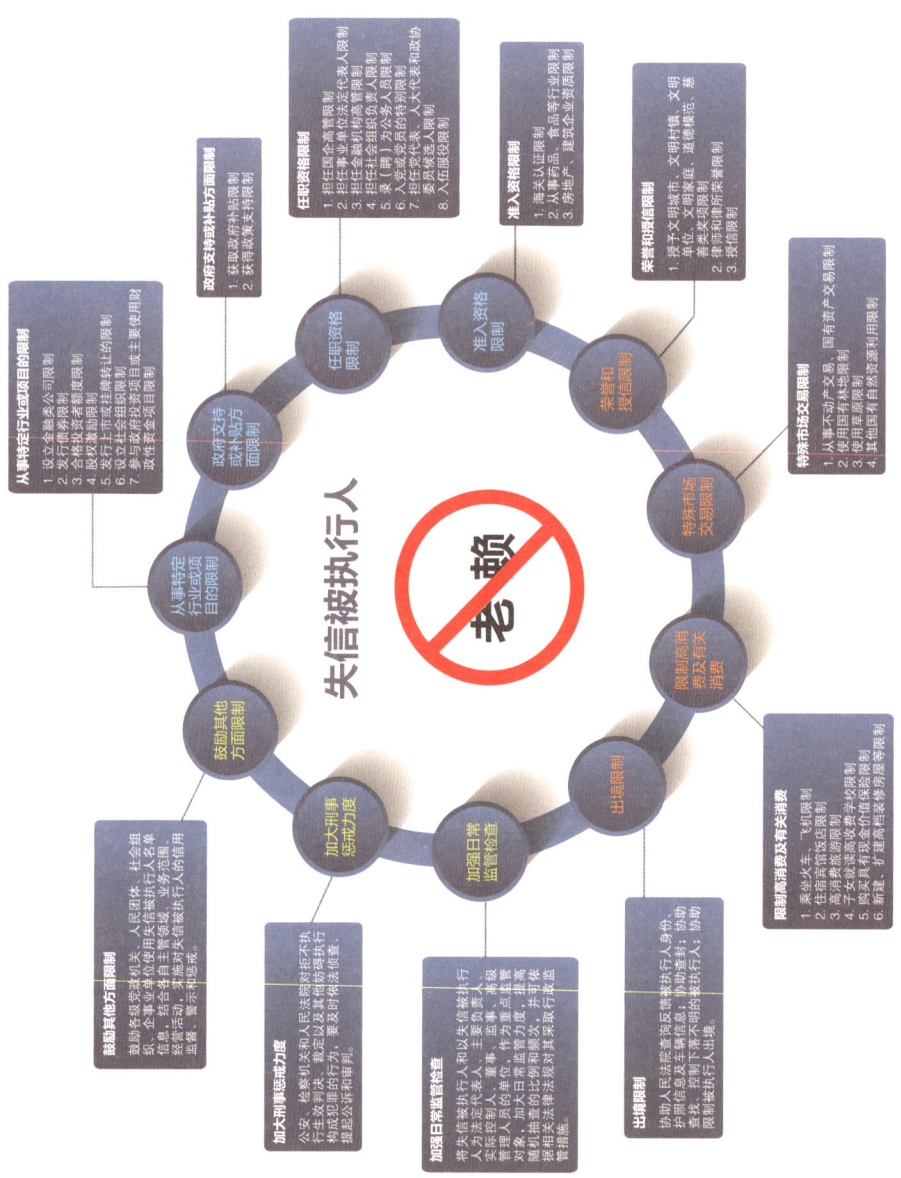

失信被执行人信用联合惩戒示意图

——**全面推行网络司法拍卖**。为克服传统拍卖方式存在的诸多弊端，最高人民法院在吸收、总结地方法院网络司法拍卖经验的基础上，在全国范围确立以网络拍卖为原则、传统拍卖为例外的司法拍卖新模式，印发网络拍卖司法解释，从 2017 年 1 月 1 日开始，在全国法院全面推行网络司法拍卖，并完善相关配套制度。截至目前，全面实行网络拍卖的法院达到 3260 个，法院覆盖率为 92.5%，网络拍卖数量占整个司法拍卖的 80% 以上。实行网络司法拍卖以来，成交率、溢价率成倍增长，流拍率、降价率、拍卖成本明显下降，有效祛除权力寻租空间，斩断不法利益链条，实现了拍卖环节违纪违法"零投诉"。从 2017 年 3 月网络拍卖系统上线至 2018 年 12 月，全国法院网络拍卖 94 万余次，成交 27 万余件，成交额 6049 亿元，标的物成交率 70.8%，溢价率 64.3%，为当事人节约佣金 186 亿元。针对司法拍卖评估环节效率低问题，创设当事人议价、定向询价、网络询价和委托评估等形式多样的评估方式，建立统一网络评估平台，提升评估规范化、信息化水平，提高财产处置效率，减轻当事人负担。

——**完善执行管理制度机制**。2013 年以来，最高人民法院狠抓执行规范体系建设，共印发 55 项重要司法解释和规范性文件，全面规范执行工作。特别是 2016 年以来，密集印发涉及财产保全、财产调查、执行和解、执行担保、先予仲裁等 37 个重要司法解释和规范性文件，加强制度建设，织密规则体系，有效约束和规范执行权。自 2014 年开始，全国法院对近 20 年来未实际执结的执行案件进行全面清查核录，把 1600 余万案件录入执行案件管理系统，为实现执行案件有序、精准、全面、智能管理打下基础。建立全国四级法院"统一管理、统一协调、统一指挥"的执行管理新模式，实现执行管理扁平化、集约化、可视化、规范化、智慧化。建成四级法院统一的执行办案平台，全国执行干警在一个平台办案，规范了执行办案标准和流程，强化了关键节点管控。建立完善四级法院统一的执行指挥管理平台，该平台具有执行协作、款物管理、申诉信访、流程监督等近20项功能，实现"一站式"执行公开、"一键式"案件督办。针对执行信访管理督办难题，将执行信访全部纳入执行管理平台，办理过程全程留痕、实时跟踪、精准管理。

——深化执行体制机制改革。积极稳妥推进人民法院内部审判权和执行权相分离改革试点。最高人民法院印发立审执工作协调运行的意见，加强立案、审判、执行、保全程序中的机制衔接。建立以法官为主导，法官助理、书记员、司法警察等司法辅助人员组成的团队化执行工作模式，实现执行人力资源效用最大化。全面推广由保险公司为申请人提供财产保全责任保险的做法，解决财产保全申请人难以提供保全担保的突出问题，提升财产保全适用率。针对司法救助金额不足的情况，最高人民法院在批准宁波法院积极试点的基础上，探索在全国范围内引入保险机制，拓展资金来源，2018年发放司法救助金6.5亿元。

七、深化司法公开和司法民主

阳光是最好的"防腐剂"。2013年以来，最高人民法院统筹谋划、一体部署，坚持依法公开、主动公开、全面公开、实质公开，同步推进审判流程、庭审活动、裁判文书、执行信息四大公开平台建设，促进司法公开透明。坚持以公开为原则、以不公开为例外，将司法公开覆盖人民法院审判执行工作各领域、各环节，确保向社会公开一切依法应当公开的内容。2018年11月，最高人民法院印发关于进一步深化司法公开的意见，不断拓展司法公开的广度和深度。

——推进审判流程公开。2014年11月，中国审判流程信息公开网正式开通，现已成为全国法院审理案件的审判流程信息的集中汇聚和统一发布平台，为全国法院审判案件的当事人提供"一站式"公开服务。案件当事人及其诉讼代理人自案件受理之日起，可以凭有效证件号码随时登录查询、下载相关案件的流程信息、材料等，程序性诉讼文书可以通过网络电子送达。2018年3月，最高人民法院印发关于人民法院通过互联网公开审判流程信息的规定，明确除涉及国家秘密以及法律规定应当保密或者限制获取的审判流程信息以外，人民法院审判刑事、民事、行政、国家赔偿案件过程中产生的程序性信息、处理诉讼事项的流程信息、诉讼文书、笔录等四大类审判流程信息，均应当通过互联网向参加诉讼的当事人及其法定代理人、诉讼代理人、辩护人公开。截至2018年12月底，中国审判流程信息公开网公开案件4609074件，公开率为99.43%，公开信息项数量229377909个，网站访问量 34530649 次，共推送短信 18145449 条，全国法院共发布公众栏目信息数量 1536570 个。

——推进庭审活动公开。2013 年 12 月 11 日，中国法院庭审直播网开通。2016 年 9 月，最高人民法院在对中国庭审直播网全面升级的基础上，正式开通中国庭审公开网，实现了各级人民法院庭审视频的统一汇集和权威发布。自 2016 年 7 月 1 日起，最高人民法院所有依法公开开庭的案件均可以通过互联网进行庭审直播。社会公众可以通过该网实时选择观看全国法院正在直播的案件、点播观看庭审录像、获取庭审直播统计信息，并且还可以通过微博、微信进行收藏和分享，真正实现了庭审信息的全面覆盖、实时互联和深度公开。截至 2018 年底，中国庭审公开网累计直播庭审 230 万余件，点击率超过 138 亿人次。各级人民法院高度重视大案要案审判公开，通过微博、互联网直播等方式，直播"加百利"轮海难救助再审案、"乔丹"商标争议行政纠纷系列案等一批社会关注的重大案件庭审实况。2016 年 1 月 7 日至 8 日，北京市海淀区人民法院全程直播"快播"涉嫌传播淫秽物品牟利案件庭审，直播总时长达 20 余小时，直播期间累计有 100 余万人观看视频，27 条长微博全程播报庭审情况，累计阅读次数达 3600 余万次。

——推进裁判文书公开。2013 年 11 月，最高人民法院开通中国裁判文书网，建立全国统一的裁判文书公开平台，并率先在该网公布本院作出的裁判文书。2014 年 1 月 1 日起，各级人民法院的生效裁判文书陆续在中国裁判文书网公布。2015 年 12 月，中国裁判文书网改版，增加一键智能查询、关联文书查询、个性化服务等功能，实现少数民族语言裁判文书的公开，开通蒙、藏、维、朝鲜和哈萨克等五种民族语言文书的浏览和下载功能。2016 年 8 月 30 日，中国裁判文书网 APP 手机客户端正式上线。2016 年 8 月起，中国裁判文书网每日访问量均超过 2000 万次。2016 年 8 月 29 日，最高人民法院发布修订后的关于人民法院在互联网公布裁判文书的规定，详细列举了应当公开的裁判文书类型，除涉及国家秘密、未成年人犯罪、以调解方式结案或者确认人民调解协议效力、离婚诉讼或者涉及未成年子女抚养、监护的文书以外，其他裁判文书一律在互联网公布。涉及个人隐私的裁判文书在隐去涉及个人隐私的内容后上网公开，已上诉、抗诉的一审裁判文书也应当上网公开，同时与二审裁判文书建立有机关联。对于不公开的裁判文书，除可能泄露国家秘密的以外，公布案号、审理法院、裁判日期及不公开的理由。将裁判文书公开工作模式由传统的专门机构集中公布模式转变为办案法官在办案平台一键点击自动公布模式，建立了对公众反馈的投诉和意见处理机制、裁判文书公开督导机制，充分接受社会各界对裁判文书公开工作的监督。截至 2018 年底，中国裁判文书网公开裁判文书已经超过 6200 万份，网站访问量突破 210 亿次，用户覆盖全球 210 多个国家和地区，已成为全世界最大的裁判文书数据资源库。

——推进执行信息公开。2014 年 11 月，最高人民法院将被执行人信息、全国法院失信被执行人名单、执行案件流程信息、执行裁判文书四项公开信息予以整合，统一纳入中国执行信息公开网，实现全国法院执行案件信息、失信被执行人信息、终结本次执行案件信息、网络司法拍卖信息等内容统一、及时、自动公开。2016 年 9 月 14 日，最高人民法院"中国执行"微信公众号正式上线，开通执行信息查询、执行规范发布、法律法规解读、执行文书公开等功能，方便社会公众随时随地获取执行工作信息和享受司法服务。截至 2018 年底，执行信息公开平台累计公布失信被执行人 1288 万人次。

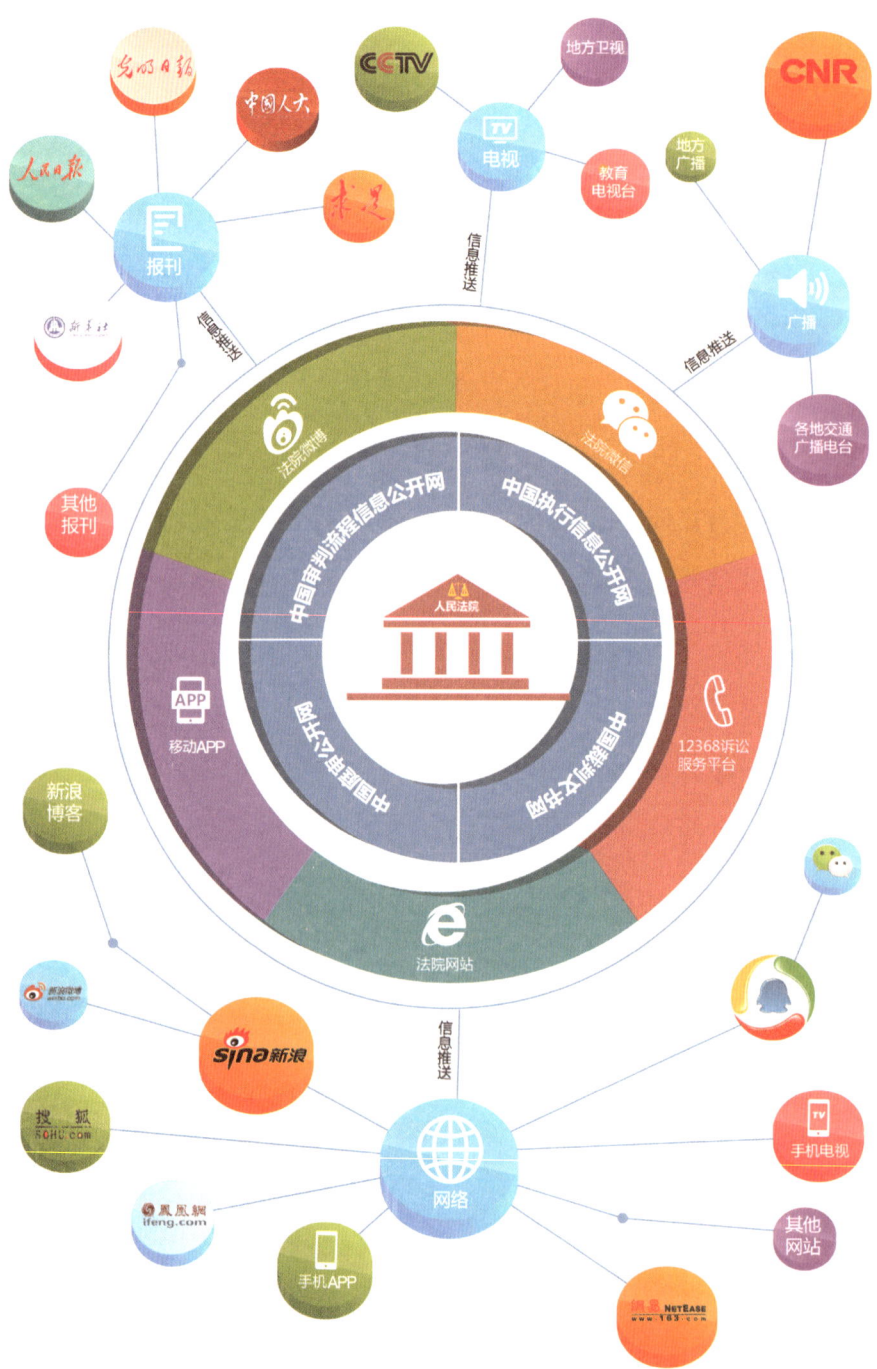

中国法院司法公开机制全景图

人民法院四大司法公开平台界面图

　　——推进企业破产信息公开。2016 年 8 月，最高人民法院发布关于企业破产案件信息公开的规定，正式开通全国企业破产重整案件信息网，成为对破产案件各类信息分级进行发布的互联网资讯平台，法律文书、管理人招募公告、投资人招募公告、资产拍卖公告等公告信息同步在该网公布，为债权人、债务人企业、市场投资者、其他利害关系人提供在线司法服务。2018 年，通过全国企业破产重整案件信息网公开的破产案件数量达 29856 件。

　　——拓展司法公开广度和深度。最高人民法院定期发布《最高人民法院公报》《最高人民法院工作报告》《人民法院工作年度报告（中英文）》，发布中国知识产权司法保护状况白皮书、海事审判白皮书、环境资源审判白皮书、行政审判白皮书、司法改革白皮书、司法公开白皮书等，面向国内外公开司法文件、重大案件和法院工作情况。成立司法案例研究院并开通中国司法案例网，运用大数据技术和互联网，汇集发布大量中外案例，智能生成具有公众认可度的典型案例，推动形成清晰明确的社会指引。中国司法案例网通过热点直击、案例方法、案例论坛等栏目，引领广大法律职业共同体成员，参与司法案例收集、生成、研究和交流，努力构建案例研究新平台。各级人民法院通过建设法院政务网站、法院微博微信、移动新闻客户端、院长信箱、代表委员联络平台、主题开放日活动等，进一步深化司法公开。

2014 年 12 月 31 日，最高人民法院政务网站全面改版，开通诉讼服务网，方便当事人咨询查询、预约立案、网上阅卷、联系法官。2015 年 12 月 15 日，最高人民法院开通英文网站。自 2013 年起，最高人民法院先后开通新浪官方微博、腾讯微博、人民微博，上线全国法院微博发布厅，全面进驻国内主流微博平台。截至 2018 年底，三个官方微博订户总数达 5795.3 万余人，发布微博 4.4 万条，被转发、评论 508.4 万条。2013 年 11 月，最高人民法院官方微信正式上线，截至 2018 年底，已发布 3909 期图文消息，订阅用户 104.4 万人。2015 年 1 月起，全国法院开始实施新闻发布月度例会制度。2014 年至 2018 年，最高人民法院召开新闻发布会 114 场，共发布司法文件 76 件，通报工作进展 53 次。2015 年至 2018 年，通过召开典型案例通气会的方式，共公布典型案例 477 个。举办中国—东盟大法官论坛、金砖国家大法官论坛暨博鳌亚洲论坛环境司法分论坛、中国—中东欧国家最高法院院长会议、丝绸之路（敦煌）司法合作国际论坛、智慧法院暨网络法治论坛、中国与葡萄牙语国家最高法院院长会议、第十三次上海合作组织成员国最高法院院长会议等一系列重大司法外事活动。与 140 多个国家和地区的最高司法机关及 18 个国际组织、区域性组织建立友好交往关系，与 43 个国家的最高司法机关和 2 个国际组织签署了合作协议，讲好中国法治故事，传播中国法治声音，有力提升了中国司法的国际形象和影响力。

——改革人民陪审员制度。 2015 年 5 月，根据全国人大常委会授权，最高人民法院会同司法部印发人民陪审员制度改革试点方案和试点工作实施办法，在 10 个省（自治区、直辖市）选择 50 个法院开展为期两年的试点。试点内容包括：改革人民陪审员选任条件，完善选任方式，扩大参审范围，明确参审职权，强化职业保障，建立退出机制，发挥人民陪审员熟悉社情民意的优势，逐步实行人民陪审员不再就法律适用问题表决，只参与审理事实认定问题等。为进一步研究解决改革试点中的难点问题，2017 年 4 月，全国人大常委会决定将试点期限延长一年。2018 年 4 月，全国人大常委会审议通过最高人民法院关于人民陪审员制度改革试点情况的报告，人民陪审员制度改革试点工作顺利完成。试点工作成效显著，呈现"四个转变"：人民陪审员选任方式主要由组织推荐向随机抽选转变，人民陪审员参审职权由全面参审向只参与审理事实问题转变，人民陪审员参审方式由 3 人合议庭模式向 7 人以上大合议庭陪审机制转变，人民陪审员审理案件由注重陪审案件"数量"向关注陪审案件"质量"转变。改革后，人民陪审员来源更加广泛，结构更加合理，作用发挥更加充分。2018 年 4 月，《中华人民共和国人民陪审员法》颁布，人民陪审员制度改革试点成果上升为法律制度。司法部、最高人民法院、公安部印发人民陪审员选任办法，构建了以随机抽选为主、个人申请和组织推荐为辅的人民陪审员选任模式。

八、推进法院人员分类管理

最高人民法院按照国家统一部署，配合中央有关部门，全方位改革司法人事管理制度。

——建立司法人员分类管理制度。针对以往司法人员管理制度没有充分体现司法职业特点的问题，最高人民法院积极推进司法人员分类管理制度改革，将法院人员分为法官、审判辅助人员和司法行政人员三类，并分别实行不同的管理制度，法官、审判辅助人员、司法行政人员各归其位、各尽其责。截至 2018 年底，法官、审判辅助人员、司法行政人员比例分别为 34.6%、49.5%、15.9%。

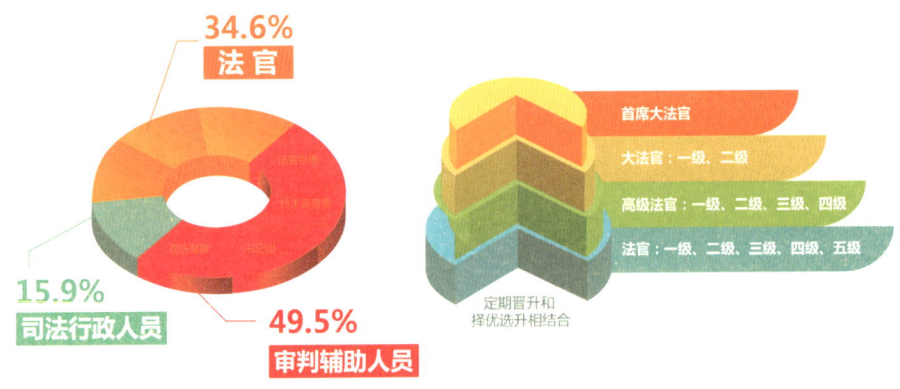

法院人员分类管理示意图

——全面实施法官员额制。全国法院按照以案定额、按岗定员、总量控制、省级统筹的原则，经过严格的考试、考核程序，从原来的21 万名法官中遴选产生 12.5 万名员额法官，主要配置在审判业务岗位，综合行政岗位一律不配备员额法官，实现了 85% 以上法院人员向办案一线集中，资源配置更加合理，队伍结构更加优化。各高级人民法院严格落实中央确定的员额比例上限，根据法院案件数量、辖区法院经济社会发展状况、人口数量等基础数据，结合法院审级职能、法官工作量、审判辅助人员配置等因素，实行三级法院的法官员额在辖区内统一调配，并向基层人民法院和人案矛盾突出地区倾斜。广东法院以案件量为主要依据，对汕头"案少人多"地区核定法官员额低于 30%，对深圳、东莞、中山等"案多人少"地区核定法官员额超过 50%。建立法官员额交流和退出机制，"有进有出、能上能下"的员额动态管理机制逐步形成。截至 2018 年 6 月，因转岗、调离、辞职、退休、考核不合格等情形，全国已有 5938 人退出员额。

——改革法官选任制度。在省一级设立由法官代表和社会有关人员参与的法官遴选委员会，制定公开、公平、公正的选任程序，确保品行端正、经验丰富、专业水平较高的优秀法律人才成为法官人选。完善法官逐级遴选制度，2016 年 5 月，中央组织部、最高人民法院、最高人民检察院印发关于建立法官检察官逐级遴选制度的意见，明确了地市级以上人民法院法官一般通过逐级遴选方式产生。2015 年 10 月，最高人民法院经过严格遴选，从全国地方法院的 62 名报名者中遴选确定 7 名优秀法官。2014 年 3 月，最高人民法院面向专家学者、律师、其他机关从事法律工作的人员，公开选拔高层次审判人才，从 195 名报名者中择优确定 5 人为选拔人选，包括专家学者、资深律师和优秀检察官。2015 年，上海法院面向社会公开选任 1 名法官，青海法院面向社会公开选任 3 名法官。上海、广东、福建等地法院已开始从优秀法官助理中遴选员额法官，并在基层人民法院任职。

——改革法官职务序列和工资福利制度。建立法官单独职务序列制度，员额法官按照单独职务序列进行管理，法官等级与行政职级脱钩，建立按期晋升、择优选升和特别选升相结合的晋升机制，实行有别于其他公务员、体现法官职业特点的人事管理制度，拓宽广大基层法官的职业发展通道，增强了法官的职业尊荣感和工作积极性。截至2018年底，全国法院均已建立员额法官单独职务序列等级确定机制，约98%的法院已开展法官等级按期晋升工作，约52%的法院已开展法官等级择优选升工作。建立了法官与单独职务序列改革相配套的工资福利制度，全国法院均已落实新的工资制度和绩效考核奖金，较大幅度提高了法官的工资水平。最高人民法院积极协调中央相关部门，明确了员额法官岗位交流、退休年龄、医疗待遇、差旅待遇、公务交通补贴等政策，以通知形式印发实施，并督促各级法院推动落实。

——改革审判辅助人员招录培养制度。最高人民法院配合中央有关部门，印发关于招录人民法院法官助理的意见，各地有序开展法官助理省级统一单独招录，稳妥推进未入额法官和符合条件的书记员转任法官助理工作，加强法官助理配备。2017年4月，最高人民法院会同财政部、人力资源和社会保障部印发聘用制书记员管理制度改革方案，着力解决聘用制书记员管理不够规范、保障水平较低、队伍不够稳定等问题。各地法院拓宽审判辅助人员的来源渠道，探索完善审判辅助人员管理培养制度，着力优化审判辅助人员结构。改革后，北京法院审判辅助人员从2689名增加到4538名，增加68.8%；上海法院法官与审判辅助人员配比从1∶0.75变为1∶1.78。江苏省高级人民法院着力推进书记员制度改革，制定书记员岗位等级标准和培训考核办法，做好书记员的定位、定员、定责工作，一线法官与书记员的配比达到1∶1.1，改变了过去多名法官共用1名书记员的情况。

——建立法律研修学者和法律实习生制度。最高人民法院建立法律研修学者制度和法律实习生制度，已接收 30 名研修学者和 313 名法律实习生，加强了与法律院校和法律科研机构司法合作交流，推动完善了法治人才培养机制。各地普遍加强同法律院校的合作，建立接收法律院校实习生担任法官助理制度，实习法官助理在法官指导下参与审判辅助工作，缓解了人民法院法官助理不足的矛盾，探索出法院人员分类管理改革新模式。四川省成都市中级人民法院与四川大学、西南财经大学、电子科技大学等 11 所高校签署实习法官助理机制合作共建协议书，探索推进在高校设置实习法官助理课程，由合作院校选派优秀在读法律专业研究生（或本科生）从事审判辅助实践，目前已累计接收 5 期 304 名法律实习生。

法院人事制度改革示意图

——**加强司法职业伦理建设**。为全面加强法官职业素养，恪守司法职业伦理，人民法院健全法官统一职业培训和入职晋级宣誓制度，完善职业道德准则、职业行为规范和职业道德评价机制。最高人民法院会同中央有关部门印发文件，禁止法院人员与当事人、律师、特殊关系人、中介组织的六种接触交往行为，要求司法人员在案件办理过程中，应当在工作场所、工作时间接待当事人、律师、特殊关系人、中介组织。司法人员从司法机关离任后，不得担任原任职单位办理案件的诉讼代理人或者辩护人。对因违法违纪被开除公职的司法人员，终身禁止从事法律职业。

九、完善司法服务保障国家发展制度机制

人民法院承担着维护国家政治安全、确保社会大局稳定、维护社会公平正义、保障人民安居乐业的重要使命。各级人民法院立足司法职能，通过加强审判执行工作，深化司法体制改革，助力推动形成更高层次改革开放新格局，营造更加稳定、公正、透明、可预期的法治营商环境。

——完善国家重大发展战略司法服务和保障机制。最高人民法院印发关于为改善营商环境提供司法保障的文件，北京、上海两市高级人民法院也完善相关司法政策，致力于打造法治化国际营商环境。在世界银行发布的《2019 年营商环境报告》中，涉及司法效率、司法成本、审判组织、司法程序、信息化程度的"执行合同"指标中国得分 78.97 分，排名全球第 6 位。最高人民法院印发关于为京津冀协同发展、长江经济带发展、乡村振兴战略提供司法服务和保障的意见，创新司法协同工作机制，为国家重大战略发展提供司法服务和保障。完善金融审判领域风险监测预警机制，建立金融案件大数据资源库，健全金融风险防范信息共享机制。

——健全完善"一带一路"国际商事争端解决机制。2018 年 6 月，最高人民法院印发关于设立国际商事法庭的司法解释，配套制定国际商事专家委员会工作规则、国际商事法庭程序指引等规定。国际商事法庭可以委托国际商事专家委员会成员、国际商事调解机构对国际商事争议进行调解，支持具备条件、在国际上享有良好声誉的国内仲裁

机构开展涉"一带一路"国际商事仲裁，形成调解、仲裁与诉讼有机衔接、功能互补的国际商事多元纠纷解决机制。2018年6月29日，最高人民法院第一国际商事法庭和第二国际商事法庭先后在深圳、西安揭牌，开始正式办公。

——完善产权司法保护机制。2016年11月，最高人民法院印发关于充分发挥审判职能作用切实加强产权司法保护的意见，对完善产权司法保护工作作出全面部署。人民法院坚持平等保护、全面保护、依法保护理念，对各类产权主体的诉讼地位和法律适用一视同仁，严格区分经济纠纷与刑事犯罪，坚决防止把经济纠纷当作犯罪处理。最高人民法院发布两批保护产权和企业家合法权益典型案例，依法甄别纠正张文中案等涉产权冤错案件，取得良好社会效果。

——加强知识产权审判领域改革创新。2017年11月，十九届中央深改组第一次会议审议通过《关于加强知识产权审判领域改革创新若干问题的意见》，提出完善符合知识产权审判特点的权利效力审查机制和证据规则，建立体现知识产权价值的侵权损害赔偿制度，完善知识产权审判体系。2017年4月20日，最高人民法院印发《中国知识产权司法保护纲要（2016—2020）》，明确了知识产权司法保护工作的基本原则、主要目标和重点措施。2016年7月，最高人民法院印发关于在全国法院推进知识产权民事、行政和刑事案件审判"三合一"工作的意见，各级人民法院的知识产权审判部门统一更名为知识产权审判庭，积极推进知识产权审判庭统一审理知识产权民事、行政和刑事案件。

——完善生态环境资源司法保护制度机制。最高人民法院印发文件，为全面加强生态文明建设与绿色发展提供司法保障。各地加强环境资源审判专门化建设，2014年6月，最高人民法院设立环境资源审判庭，截至2018年12月底，22个高级人民法院，110个中级人民法院和 257 个基层人民法院设立环境资源专门审判机构。全国法院共设立环境资源审判庭、合议庭或者巡回法庭 1270 个，其中环境资源审判庭 390 个，专门合议庭 808 个，巡回法庭 72 个。按照生态环境损害赔偿制度改革试点方案要求，积极探索省级政府提起生态环境损害赔偿诉讼案件的审理规则。截至 2018 年，全国法院共受理 20 件生态环境损害赔偿案件和司法确认案件。

十、完善司法管理体制和案件管辖制度

2014 年以来，最高人民法院配合中央有关部门，推动司法管理体制改革，调整案件管辖制度，完善维护司法权威制度，推动形成信赖司法、尊重司法、支持司法的制度环境和社会氛围。

——**推动省级以下地方法院人财物统一管理**。改革司法管理体制，推动省级以下地方法院人财物统一管理，彰显司法权的中央事权属性。各地依托省级平台，以公开、透明、民主方式推进统管工作。省级以下地方法院机构编制实行由省级机构编制部门管理为主、高级人民法院协同管理的体制，市县两级机构编制部门不再承担法院机构编制管理工作。各地建立省级以下地方法院法官统一由省级提名、管理并按法定程序任免的机制。法官助理由省级公务员主管部门会同高级人民法院统一招录。初任法官人选由省一级法官遴选委员会在专业上进行把关，统一由省级提名并按法定程序任免。各地因地制宜探索省级以下地方法院经费统一管理体制改革，北京、天津、山西等 18 个省、自治区、直辖市和大连、深圳 2 个计划单列市实行省级以下地方法院所需经费省级统一管理，省、市、县三级法院均为省级政府财政部门的一级预算单位，向省级政府财政部门编报预算，预算资金通过国库集中支付系统拨付。

——**完善审级制度**。为适应经济社会发展需要，合理定位四级法院职能，最高人民法院调整了高级人民法院和中级人民法院管辖第一审民商事案件的标准，提高了基层人民法院一审民商事案件管辖诉讼标的额标准。对重大疑难、新类型和在适用法律上有普遍意义的案件，可以由上级人民法院自行决定由其审理，或者根据下级人民法院报请决定由其审理。2015 年 2 月，最高人民法院就民事审判监督程序严格依法适用指令再审和发回重审相关问题印发司法解释，统一指令再审和提审的标准，严格禁止随意发回重审，要求上级人民法院裁定指令再审、发回重审的，应当在裁定书中阐明指令再审或者发回重审的具体理由。

——开展行政案件跨行政区划集中管辖改革试点。针对行政案件原则上由被告行政机关所在地法院管辖、可能受到当地行政机关干预的问题，各地法院按照中央统一部署，探索建立与行政区划适当分离的行政案件管辖制度，通过提级管辖、异地交叉管辖、相对集中管辖等多种形式，探索各具特色的管辖制度改革，切实解决行政诉讼立案难、审理难、执行难等突出问题。2015 年 6 月，最高人民法院发布关于跨行政区域集中管辖行政案件的意见，指导部分高级人民法院根据本地实际，确定若干法院跨行政区划管辖行政案件，整合行政审判资源，促进改善行政审判司法环境。福建、山东、河南、广东、湖北、湖南等高级人民法院以统一指定方式，将部分一审行政案件交给原管辖法院之外的基层人民法院或者中级人民法院管辖，通过依法公正审理各类行政诉讼案件，消除了群众对地方保护主义的顾虑。

——完善环境资源案件归口审理和集中管辖制度。各级人民法院积极探索构建环境资源民事、行政、刑事案件归口审理模式。最高人民法院环境资源审判庭实行环境资源民事、行政案件"二合一"归口审理。江苏、福建等 16 家高级人民法院实行环境资源民事、行政案件"二合一"或刑事、民事、行政案件"三合一"的归口审理模式。各地法院结合本地区环境资源保护特点，探索环境资源案件跨行政区划集中管辖模式。江苏、河南、海南、湖北等高级人民法院探索以流域、海域等生态系统或生态功能区为单位集中管辖环境资源案件，推动案件管辖和审理模式更加符合生态环境自身特点和规律，切实防止地方保护主义，加大生态环境保护力度。

——健全行政机关负责人依法出庭应诉制度。2016 年 7 月，最高人民法院印发通知，要求各级人民法院根据《中华人民共和国行政诉讼法》相关规定，进一步规范和促进行政应诉工作。对于行政机关负责人和行政机关相应的工作人员均不出庭，仅委托律师出庭的；或者人民法院书面建议行政机关负责人出庭应诉，行政机关负责人不出庭应诉的，人民法院应当记录在案并在裁判文书中载明，可以依法予以公告，并建议任免机关、监察机关或者上一级行政机关对相关责任人员严肃处理。江苏省行政机关负责人行政诉讼出庭应诉率连续两年稳定在 90% 以上，南通等 9 个地级市的行政机关负责人出庭应诉率超过90%，昆山等 59 个县（市、区）达到 100%，海安县人民政府连续三任县长出庭应诉，连续六年行政机关负责人出庭应诉率达到 100%。

——完善维护诉讼诚信和司法权威的制度。最高人民法院配合全国人民代表大会常务委员会，推动修改刑法相关罪名，进一步维护司法权威。2015 年 8 月 29 日通过的《中华人民共和国刑法修正案（九）》完善了拒不执行判决、裁定罪，增加一档法定刑，并增加单位犯罪的规定；修改了扰乱法庭秩序罪，将殴打诉讼参与人以及侮辱、诽谤、威胁司法工作人员或者诉讼参与人，不听法庭制止等严重扰乱法庭秩序的行为增列为犯罪；增设了虚假诉讼罪，将以捏造的事实提起民事诉讼，妨害司法秩序或者严重侵害他人合法权益的行为增列为犯罪。2016 年 6 月，最高人民法院印发关于防范和制裁虚假诉讼的指导意见，指导各地识别虚假诉讼要素，加大审查力度，坚决予以制裁，维护诉讼诚信和秩序。

十一、推进智慧法院建设

2013 年以来，人民法院认真贯彻落实创新驱动战略、网络强国战略、大数据战略和新一代人工智能发展规划，全面加强智慧法院建设，网络化、阳光化、智能化应用全面发展，人民法院信息化 3.0 版的主体框架已然确立，有力促进了审判体系和审判能力现代化。

——**加强信息化建设顶层规划和标准制定**。最高人民法院印发《人民法院信息化建设五年发展规划（2016—2020）》，明确智慧法院建设的重点任务和具体要求。按照"系统工程、标准先行"的指导思想，最高人民法院健全人民法院信息化标准体系，编制发布以案件数据标准为核心的 85 项技术标准，支撑各级人民法院信息资源共享交换、系统研发、信息安全和质效型运维体系建设。印发人民法院案件案号的若干规定及配套标准、人民法院案件信息业务标准（2015）等标准化文件，对全国 3500 余个法院进行代码化处理，构建起三层级案件类型体系，为构建案件信息新型标准体系奠定了坚实基础。

——**加强信息化基础设施和保障体系建设**。各级人民法院不断升级完善法院专网、移动专网、外部专网、互联网和涉密内网五大网系，支持人民法院全业务网上办理。全国所有 3500 多个法院、1 万多个派出法庭全部接入法院专网。全国已建成 2.8 万多个科技法庭，实现多媒体证据展示、远程审判、庭审录音录像、庭审语音自动识别等功能。最高人民法院率先提出并建立质效型运维保障体系，建成并运用可视化运维管理工具，横向覆盖五大网系，纵向贯穿基础设施、业务应用、数据管理、信息安全、运维保障五个层次。

——**全面推进电子诉讼**。为适应互联网时代发展要求，推进诉讼模式和机制创新，各级人民法院大力推进电子诉讼，推动诉讼活动全程网络化。最高人民法院指导推动全国法院部署网上立案、网上缴费、网上证据交换、网上开庭、电子送达等五个标准模块，吉林、浙江、江苏等地法院已经全面建成并广泛应用。浙江省率先在宁波市试点进而在全省推开"移动微法院"建设，打造依托微信小程序的一站式移动诉讼平台，当事人可以实现网上立案、查询、调解、庭审、执行、缴费等20余项事项的办理。浙江省宁波市两级法院使用"移动微法院"办理的一审民商案件平均审理用时减少17天，执行案件平均用时减少28天，当事人反映"找法官难"的投诉数量下降近30%。

——**开发应用刑事审判智能辅助系统**。根据中央关于推进以审判为中心的诉讼制度改革的部署，上海开发刑事审判智能辅助办案系统，创造性地运用大数据、云计算、人工智能等现代科技手段，制定统一适用的证据标准、证据规则并嵌入公安、检察、法院、司法行政各机关的刑事办案系统中，帮助公安、检察、法院办案人员依法、全面、规范收集和审查证据，确保侦查、审查起诉的案件事实证据经得起法律检验，确保刑事办案过程全程可视、全程留痕、全程监督，以减少司法任意性，有效防范冤假错案产生。

——**加强案件审理和司法管理的智能化辅助**。2016年8月，最高人民法院印发关于全面推进人民法院电子卷宗随案同步生成和深度应用的指导意见，推动案件卷宗随案电子化并上传办案系统，为法官网上办案实质化、审判辅助智能化创造条件。最高人民法院依托大数据管理和服务平台汇聚全国法院案件卷宗信息，为法院之间电子卷宗调阅奠定技术基础。最高人民法院建设"法信"平台，打造国内领先、世界一流的东方法律信息服务品牌，汇聚各类法律知识资源、案例、专业知识和成果，为法官、律师、学者、社会公众等不同群体按需提供全面、便捷、智能的法律知识资源检索、智推服务。各地开发应用庭审语音识别系统，自动区分庭审发言对象及发言内容，将语音自动转化为文字。江苏省苏州市中级人民法院已经使用该系统支持开庭2.7万余次，语音识别正确率已达到90%以上，庭审时间平均缩短20%至30%。

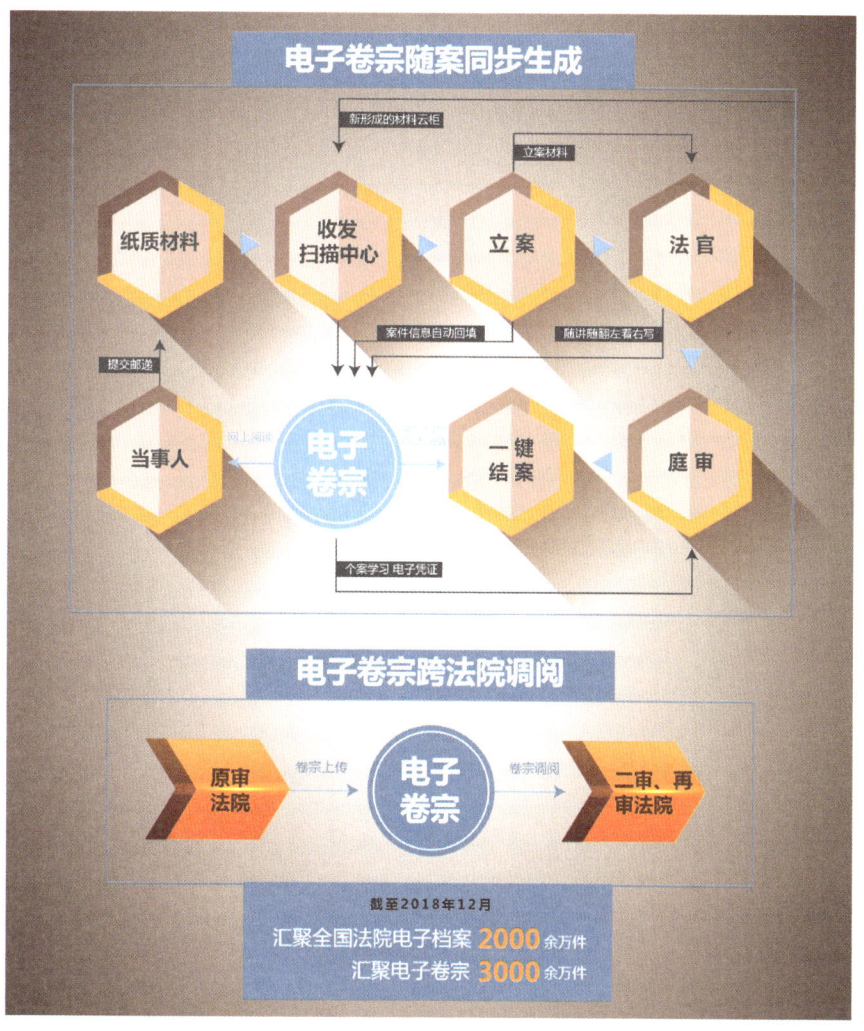

电子卷宗随案同步生成示意图

——**信息化、大数据服务司法管理和决策。**最高人民法院建成人民法院大数据管理和服务平台，实现对全国法院司法信息资源的汇集、管理、分析和服务。人民法院大数据管理和服务平台实时收集全国法院收结案数据，每5分钟自动更新一次，每日大约汇聚7万至8万个案件数据，目前成为全世界最大的审判信息资源库，并支持对全国法院收结案情况、案由分布等进行分析。2016年，全国法院全面实现司法统计与大数据管理和服务平台并轨，标志着人民法院彻底告别人工司法统计时代。针对定量化人事绩效评估需求，大数据管理和服务平台对汇集的人事数据和案件数据进行关联融合，司法人事管理从定性到定量实现质的跨越。

结束语

　　新一轮司法体制改革始终坚持问题导向和目标导向，从影响司法公正、制约司法能力的深层次问题改起，从解决人民最关心最直接最现实的利益问题入手；始终坚持遵循司法规律与立足中国国情相结合，走中国特色司法体制改革之路，着力建设和完善中国特色社会主义司法制度；始终坚持循序渐进、依法有序推进改革，走顶层设计与试点探索相结合之路，确保改革依法积极稳妥开展。

　　人民的理解支持是司法改革的动力源泉，人民的获得感是司法改革的评价标准。面对时代的新挑战、人民的新期待、科技的新进步，中国法院的司法改革只有进行时，没有完成时。下一步，人民法院将以习近平新时代中国特色社会主义思想为指导，高举新时代改革开放伟大旗帜，紧紧围绕努力让人民群众在每一个司法案件中感受到公平正义的目标，推动公正高效权威的中国特色社会主义司法制度更加成熟更加定型，全面提升司法能力、司法效能和司法公信，推动营造更加良好的社会主义法治环境，创造更高水平的社会主义司法文明，努力让人民群众在每一个司法案件中感受到公平正义。

人民法院主要司法改革文件总览图（一）

1 全面落实司法责任制

- 《最高人民法院关于完善人民法院司法责任制的若干意见》〔法发〔2015〕13号〕
- 《最高人民法院关于进一步全面落实司法责任制的实施意见》〔法发〔2018〕23号〕
- 《人民法院落实〈领导干部干预司法活动、插手具体案件处理的记录、通报和责任追究规定〉的实施办法》〔法发〔2015〕10号〕
- 《人民法院落实〈司法机关内部人员过问案件的记录和责任追究规定〉的实施办法》〔法发〔2015〕11号〕
- 《最高人民法院、最高人民检察院关于建立法官、检察官惩戒制度的意见（试行）》〔法发〔2016〕24号〕

- 《人民法院落实〈保护司法人员依法履行法定职责规定〉的实施办法》〔法发〔2017〕4号〕
- 《最高人民法院关于加强各级人民法院院长办理案件工作的意见（试行）》〔法发〔2017〕10号〕
- 《最高人民法院关于落实司法责任制 完善审判监督管理机制的意见（试行）》〔法发〔2017〕11号〕
- 《最高人民法院关于健全完善人民法院主审法官会议工作机制的指导意见（试行）》〔法发〔2018〕21号〕
- 《最高人民法院关于〈最高人民法院关于案例指导工作的规定〉实施细则》〔法〔2015〕130号〕

2 推进法院组织体系和内设机构改革

- 《最高人民法院关于北京、上海、广州知识产权法院案件管辖的规定》〔法释〔2014〕12号〕
- 《最高人民法院关于巡回法庭审理案件若干问题的规定》〔法释〔2015〕3号〕
- 《最高人民法院关于设立国际商事法庭若干问题的规定》〔法释〔2018〕11号〕
- 《最高人民法院关于上海金融法院案件管辖的规定》〔法释〔2018〕14号〕

- 《最高人民法院关于互联网法院审理案件若干问题的规定》〔法释〔2018〕16号〕
- 《最高人民法院关于知识产权法庭若干问题的规定》〔法释〔2018〕22号〕
- 《中央机构编制委员会办公室、最高人民法院关于积极推进省以下人民法院内设机构改革工作的通知》〔法〔2018〕8号〕
- 《中央机构编制委员会办公室、最高人民法院关于印发〈省以下人民法院内设机构改革试点方案〉的通知》〔法〔2016〕282号〕

3 强化人权司法保障制度机制

- 《最高人民法院关于建立健全防范刑事冤假错案工作机制的意见》〔法发〔2013〕11号〕
- 《最高人民法院关于办理减刑、假释案件具体应用法律的规定》〔法释〔2016〕23号〕
- 《最高人民法院关于常见犯罪的量刑指导意见》〔法发〔2017〕7号〕
- 《最高人民法院关于依法切实保障律师诉讼权利的规定》〔法发〔2015〕16号〕
- 《最高人民法院、最高人民检察院、公安部、国家安全部、司法部关于推进以审判为中心的刑事诉讼制度改革的意见》〔法发〔2016〕18号〕
- 《最高人民法院关于全面推进以审判为中心的刑事诉讼制度改革的实施意见》〔法发〔2017〕5号〕

- 《最高人民法院、最高人民检察院、公安部、国家安全部、司法部关于办理刑事案件严格排除非法证据若干问题的规定》〔法发〔2017〕15号〕
- 《最高人民法院关于印发〈人民法院办理刑事案件庭前会议规程（试行）〉〈人民法院办理刑事案件排除非法证据规程（试行）〉〈人民法院办理刑事案件第一审普通程序法庭调查规程（试行）〉的通知》〔法发〔2017〕31号〕
- 《最高人民法院、最高人民检察院、公安部、司法部关于在部分地区开展刑事案件速裁程序试点工作的办法》〔法〔2014〕220号〕
- 《最高人民法院、最高人民检察院、公安部、国家安全部、司法部关于在部分地区开展刑事案件认罪认罚从宽制度试点工作的办法》〔法〔2016〕386号〕
- 《最高人民法院关于全面深入推进刑事案件认罪认罚从宽制度试点工作的通知》〔法〔2018〕114号〕

4 完善司法便民利民制度机制

- 《最高人民法院关于人民法院登记立案若干问题的规定》〔法释〔2015〕8号〕
- 《最高人民法院关于人民法院特邀调解的规定》〔法释〔2016〕14号〕
- 《最高人民法院关于进一步推进涉诉信访工作机制改革的若干意见》〔法发〔2014〕3号〕
- 《最高人民法院关于进一步加强新形势下人民法庭工作的若干意见》〔法发〔2014〕21号〕
- 《最高人民法院关于全面推进人民法院诉讼服务中心建设的指导意见》〔法发〔2014〕23号〕
- 《最高人民法院关于人民法院推行立案登记制改革的意见》〔法发〔2015〕6号〕

- 《最高人民法院关于人民法院进一步深化多元化纠纷解决机制改革的意见》〔法发〔2016〕14号〕
- 《最高人民法院关于加强和规范人民法院国家司法救助工作的意见》〔法发〔2016〕16号〕
- 《最高人民法院关于进一步推进案件繁简分流优化司法资源配置的若干意见》〔法发〔2016〕21号〕
- 《最高人民法院关于民商事案件繁简分流和调解速裁操作规程（试行）》〔法发〔2017〕14号〕
- 《最高人民法院、最高人民检察院、司法部关于逐步实行律师代理申诉制度的意见》〔法发〔2017〕8号〕
- 《最高人民法院关于进一步加强民事送达工作的若干意见》〔法发〔2017〕19号〕
- 《最高人民法院关于进一步深化家事审判方式和工作机制改革的意见（试行）》〔法发〔2018〕12号〕

人民法院主要司法改革文件总览图（一）

人民法院主要司法改革文件总览图（二）

10 推进智慧法院建设

- 《人民法院信息化建设五年发展规划（2016—2020）》（法〔2016〕66号）
- 《最高人民法院关于全面推进人民法院电子卷宗随案同步生成和深度应用的指导意见》（法〔2016〕264号）
- 《最高人民法院关于加快建设智慧法院的意见》（法发〔2017〕12号）
- 《最高人民法院关于进一步加快推进电子卷宗随案同步生成和深度应用工作的通知》（法〔2018〕21号）

9 完善司法管理体制和案件管辖制度

- 《最高人民法院关于民事审判监督程序严格依法适用指令再审和发回重审若干问题的规定》（法释〔2015〕7号）
- 《最高人民法院关于海事诉讼管辖问题的规定》（法释〔2016〕2号）
- 《最高人民法院关于海事法院受理案件范围的规定》（法释〔2016〕4号）
- 《最高人民法院、最高人民检察院关于办理虚假诉讼刑事案件适用法律若干问题的解释》（法释〔2018〕17号）
- 《最高人民法院关于调整高级人民法院和中级人民法院管辖第一审民商事案件标准的通知》（法发〔2015〕7号）
- 《最高人民法院关于人民法院跨行政区域集中管辖行政案件的指导意见》（法释〔2015〕8号）
- 《最高人民法院关于防范和制裁虚假诉讼的指导意见》（法发〔2016〕13号）
- 《最高人民法院关于调整部分高级人民法院和中级人民法院管辖第一审商事案件标准的通知》（法发〔2018〕13号）
- 《最高人民法院关于行政诉讼应诉若干问题的通知》（法〔2016〕260号）

8 完善司法服务保障国家发展制度机制

- 《最高人民法院、最高人民检察院关于检察公益诉讼案件适用法律若干问题的解释》（法释〔2018〕6号）
- 《最高人民法院关于为京津冀协同发展提供司法服务和保障的意见》（法发〔2016〕5号）
- 《最高人民法院关于为长江经济带发展提供司法服务和保障的意见》（法发〔2016〕8号）
- 《最高人民法院关于充分发挥审判职能作用为推进生态文明建设与绿色发展提供司法服务和保障的意见》（法发〔2016〕12号）
- 《最高人民法院关于充分发挥审判职能作用切实加强产权司法保护的意见》（法发〔2016〕27号）
- 《最高人民法院关于为改善营商环境提供司法保障的若干意见》（法发〔2017〕23号）
- 《最高人民法院〈关于印发知识产权司法保护纲要（2016—2020）〉的通知》（法发〔2017〕13号）
- 《最高人民法院关于充分发挥审判职能作用 为企业家创新创业营造良好法治环境的通知》（法〔2018〕1号）
- 《最高人民法院关于深入学习贯彻习近平生态文明思想 为新时代生态环境保护提供司法服务和保障的意见》（法发〔2018〕7号）
- 《最高人民法院关于为海南全面深化改革开放提供司法服务和保障的意见》（法发〔2018〕16号）
- 《最高人民法院关于为实施乡村振兴战略提供司法服务和保障的意见》（法发〔2018〕19号）

7 推进司法人员分类管理

- 《中央组织部、中央政法委、最高人民法院、最高人民检察院关于印发〈法官、检察官单独职务序列改革试点方案〉的通知》（中组发〔2015〕19号）
- 《中央组织部、最高人民法院、最高人民检察院关于招录人民法院法官助理、人民检察院检察官助理的意见》（组通字〔2015〕46号）
- 《中央组织部、最高人民法院、最高人民检察院关于建立法官检察官逐级遴选制度的意见》（组通字〔2016〕29号）
- 《中央组织部、中央政法委、最高人民法院、最高人民检察院法官助理、检察官助理和书记员职务序列改革试点方案》（组通字〔2016〕36号）
- 《最高人民法院关于建立法律研修学者制度的规定》（法〔2015〕231号）
- 《最高人民法院关于建立法律实习生制度的规定》（法〔2015〕230号）
- 《最高人民法院关于印发〈法官、审判辅助人员绩效考核及奖金分配指导意见（试行）〉的通知》（法〔2016〕323号）
- 《人民法院、人民检察院关于聘用制书记员管理制度改革方案（试行）》（法〔2017〕143号）

5 推进"基本解决执行难"

- 《最高人民法院关于公布失信被执行人名单信息的若干规定》（法释〔2013〕17号）
- 《最高人民法院关于刑事裁判涉财产部分执行的若干规定》（法释〔2014〕13号）
- 《最高人民法院关于修改〈最高人民法院关于限制被执行人高消费的若干规定〉的决定》（法释〔2015〕17号）
- 《最高人民法院关于人民法院网络司法拍卖若干问题的规定》（法释〔2016〕18号）
- 《最高人民法院关于修改〈最高人民法院关于公布失信被执行人名单信息的若干规定〉的决定》（法释〔2017〕7号）
- 《最高人民法院关于建立执行约谈机制的若干规定》（法发〔2016〕7号）
- 《最高人民法院关于落实"用两到三年时间基本解决执行难问题"的工作纲要》（法发〔2016〕10号）
- 《最高人民法院关于人民法院办理执行信访案件若干问题的意见》（法发〔2016〕15号）

6 深化司法公开和司法民主

- 《最高人民法院关于人民法院在互联网公布裁判文书的规定》（法释〔2016〕19号）
- 《最高人民法院关于人民法院通过互联网公开审判流程信息的规定》（法释〔2018〕7号）
- 《最高人民法院关于推进司法公开三大平台建设的若干意见》（法发〔2013〕13号）
- 《最高人民法院关于人民法院执行流程公开的若干意见》（法发〔2014〕18号）
- 《最高人民法院关于企业破产案件信息公开的规定（试行）》（法发〔2016〕19号）
- 《最高人民法院关于进一步深化司法公开的意见》（法发〔2018〕20号）
- 《最高人民法院关于进一步加强国家赔偿信息公开工作的若干意见》（法〔2014〕320号）
- 《最高人民法院、司法部关于印发〈人民陪审员制度改革试点方案〉的通知》（法〔2015〕100号）
- 《最高人民法院、司法部关于印发〈人民陪审员制度改革试点工作实施办法〉的通知》（法〔2015〕132号）

人民法院主要司法改革文件总览图（二）

Preface

The rule of law is the fundamental method for administering the country and managing governmental affairs, while justice is a key cornerstone of the system of rule of law. Comprehensively deepening judicial reform has great and profound implications for improving and developing the socialist judicial system with Chinese characteristics and promoting the modernization of governance system and capability in our country. Since 2013, by always taking the fundamental realities of our country into consideration and keeping pace with the times, and with the aim to make the People have a perception of fairness and justice in each judicial case, the people's courts have unswervingly and comprehensively deepened the judicial reform, and improved their trial and enforcement in an all-round way, and comprehensively enhanced the efficiency, competency, and public credibility of the judiciary, yielding notable outcomes.

I. China's Court System and Reform Process

Institutional Basis of Court Reform in China

According to the *Constitution of the People's Republic of China* and the *Organic Law of the People's Courts of the People's Republic of China*, the people's courts, as the judicial organs of the State, exercise independently the adjudicative power in accordance with laws, free from any interference by administrative organs, social organizations and individuals. The State sets up the Supreme People's Court, local people's courts at different levels, and special people's courts, such as military courts. These people's courts adjudicate civil, criminal and administrative cases and other cases prescribed by laws in accordance with the law, and carry out judicial activities, including the enforcement of civil and administrative decisions. Sole judges, collegiate panels, Trial Committees, and Compensation Committees are the judicial organs prescribed by laws.

The Supreme People's Court, as the highest trial organ of the People's Republic of China, is responsible for adjudicating various cases that have material effects nationwide or are subject to its adjudication according to law, formulating judicial interpretations, supervising and guiding the judicial work of local people's courts at different levels and special people's courts, and managing certain judicial administration work of the courts nationwide within the scope of its functions and powers as per laws.

Local people's courts consist of courts at four levels, namely the grassroots people's courts, intermediate people's courts and higher people's courts. Special people's courts consist of courts such as the military courts, maritime courts, IP courts, financial courts, etc.

A people's court at a higher level supervises the judicial work of the people's courts at the next lower level. In litigious activities, the people's courts follow the principle of open trial, collegiate panel, challenge, people's assessors and defense, and two-hearing system, etc.

Basic Process of Court Reform in China

Since the introduction of the reform and opening-up policy, along with all-round economic and social development, continuous advancement of democracy and rule of law, and the People's ever-increasing demands for and expectations of judicature, the original judicial system has become unable to adopt to the demand of new situations. As early as in the 1990s, Chinese courts started the reforms focusing on enhancing the function of court trials, expanding the openness of trials and improving judicial professionalization. Since the 15th National Congress of the Communist Party of China ("CPC"), the Supreme People's Court has initiated a series of reforms in the areas of organization and system of courts, judge system, litigation procedure, modes of trial, enforcement system, judicial management, etc., and promulgated three "Five-year Reform Program for People's Courts" in 1999, 2005 and 2009 respectively. The said three Programs served as the basis of Chinese courts reform before 2013.

The *Resolution of the Central Committee of the Communist Party of China on Major Issues Concerning Comprehensively Deepening the Reform* adopted at the 3rd Plenary Session of the 18th CCCPC set an important task of advancing rule by law in China and deepening the reform of the judicial system. The *Resolution of the Central Committee of the Communist Party of China on Major Issues Concerning Advancing the All-round Law-based Governance* adopted at the 4th Plenary Session of the 18th CCCPC set the establishment of a socialist system of laws with Chinese characteristics and the building of a socialist country under the rule of law as the overall goal of comprehensively advancing law-based governance, and put forward a series of major reform measures in ensuring formulating laws in a scientific way, enforcing laws stringently, administering justice impartially, and ensuring that everyone abides by the law. The judicial reform has become an important component of the program of comprehensively deepening the reform in China and has been included in the overall development strategy of the State.

In order to further deepening the reform of people's courts, the Supreme People's Court promulgated the *Opinions on Comprehensively Deepening the Reform of People's Courts*, putting forward 65 reform measures, which was served as the *Fourth Five-year Reform Program for People's Courts 2014-2018*, and published and implemented the Opinion on February 4, 2015. As of the end of 2018, all such 65 reform tasks had been carried out in an all-round way, 256 reform documents had been formulated. Among these reform documents, 173 were issued by the Supreme People's Court separately, 46 were issued by it jointly with the related departments of the Central Government, and 37 were formulated with its promotion or participation.

At the 19th National Congress of the CPC, major strategic arrangement was made as follows: "carry out comprehensive and integrated reform of the judicial system and enforce judicial accountability in all respects, so that the people can see in every judicial case that justice is served", which marks a new stage of the judicial system reform. Based on the realities of courts, the Supreme People's Court formulated the *Opinions on Deepening the Comprehensive and Integrated Reform of the Judicial System in the People's Courts*, namely the *Fifth Five-Year Reform Program for People's Courts 2019-2023* as an important program for instructing the people's courts to deepen the comprehensive and integrated reform of the judicial system in the next five years.

Organization and Implementation of the Court Reform in China

In early 2014, China set up the Central Leading Group for Comprehensively Deepening Reform headed by President Xi Jinping, which is in charge of designing reform on an overall basis, arranging and coordinating reforms of different sectors, pushing forward reforms as a whole and supervising the implementation of reform plans. In March 2018, it was renamed as the Central Comprehensively Deepening Reforms Commission. During the period between January 22, 2014 and December 31, 2018, the Central Leading Group for Comprehensively Deepening Reform (hereinafter referred to as "CLGCDR") and the Central Comprehensively Deepening

Reforms Commission (hereinafter referred to as "CCDRC"), in aggregate, held 45 meetings, considered and passed 35 documents relating to important reforms of people's courts.

The CCDRC has six special groups, which are responsible for considering important issues relating to reforms in the relevant areas, coordinating and advancing the formulation and implementation of special reform policies and measures. The Leading Group for Reform of the Social System (also called Central Leading Group for Reform of the Judicial System) is responsible for deepening the reform of the judicial system.

The reform of the judicial system covers a wide range of issues and has high policy sensitivity. In consideration that the basic measures of the reform of the judicial system include the improvement of classified management of judicial personnel, improvement of judicial accountability, improvement of job security of judicial personnel and promotion of centralized management of personnel, financial and material resources of local courts below the provincial level, China launched, according to the principle that major reforms shall be first conducted on a pilot basis, pilot reforms in respect of the aforesaid four issues in several provinces, autonomous regions and municipalities in three batches, to accumulate experience for advancing the reform in an all-round way. Since June 2014, the first judicial system reform pilots have been initiated in 7 provinces and municipalities, namely Shanghai, Jilin, Hubei, Guangdong, Hainan, Guizhou, and Qinghai. Since June 2015, the second judicial system reform pilots have been initiated in 11 provinces, autonomous regions and municipalities, namely Shanxi,

Inner Mongolia, Heilongjiang, Jiangsu, Zhejiang, Anhui, Fujian, Shandong, Chongqing, Yunnan, and Ningxia. Since March 2016, the third judicial system reform pilots have been initiated in Beijing and other 13 provinces, autonomous regions and municipalities and the Xinjiang Uygur Autonomous Region Production and Construction Corps. Since July 2016, these four major reforms have been implemented nationwide in an all-round way.

The Supreme People's Court set up a leading group for judicial reform headed by Zhou Qiang, Chief Justice, responsible for organizing, leading, arranging, and coordinating the judicial reform of courts, holding plenary and special meetings, overall planning of key issues of reform, considering reform proposals, discussing and deciding on major issues. Each higher people's court sets up a leading group for judicial reform, responsible for supervising, guiding, arranging, and coordinating the judicial reform of courts within its jurisdiction. Each higher people's court's proposal of pilot program for judicial reform is subject to the examination and approval by the Supreme People's Court, and in case of any program involving any major reform, by the Central Government.

II. Fully Implementing the Judicial Accountability System

It is both an objective requirement of the law of justice and a core content of the reform of the judicial system that the one who tries a case shall have the power to decide the case and be responsible for his decision. In September 2015, the Supreme People's Court promulgated the *Several Opinions of the Supreme People's Court on Improving the Judicial Accountability System of People's Courts*, establishing a new operating mechanism of adjudicative power, to instruct the courts nationwide to advance the reform of the judicial accountability system. In December 2018, the Supreme People's Court promulgated the *Opinions of the Supreme People's Court on the Further and Full Implementation of Judicial Accountability System*, providing more guidance on the issues such as improving the mechanism of trial supervision and management and the mechanism of unified application of law, to promote full implementation of the judicial accountability system. Since the full implementation of the judicial accountability system reform, in courts nationwide, the number of first-line judicial personnel has increased by over 20%, the average number of cases handled by each person has increased by over 20%, and the rate of conclusion of cases has increased by over 18%.

Implementing accountability system for sole judges and collegiate panels handling cases. Fully respecting the status of sole judges and collegiate panels as the statutory judicial organs, most of the courts at different levels have established an accountability system in which "the one who tries a case shall have the power to decide the case and be responsible for his decision", and have all but revoked the system of asking for instructions and examination and approval level by level. The written judgments formed in the course of adjudication by collegiate panels or sole judges are released upon signature by collegiate panel members or sole judges. Except the cases considered and decided by the judicial committees, court/tribunal presidents no longer review or issue any written judgment on the cases of which they have not directly participated in the trial. Since the reform, in courts nationwide, the number of cases on which the judgments are directly made by sole judges and collegiate panels has reached over 98% of the total number of cases, and the number of cases referred to judicial committees for discussion has fallen sharply. In Shanghai, for example, the ratio of the cases directly decided by the sole judges or collegiate panels has reached 99.99%, and only 0.1% of the cases concluded have been submitted to the judicial committees for discussion.

Flexibly organizing the judicial team. According to applicable laws and based on actual circumstances, the grassroots people's courts organize judicial teams with the judges as the core members, and judge assistants, clerks and other auxiliary judicial personnel as the supporting members, describe the duties of the judges, judge assistants and clerks, and improve the case handling mechanism with clear power and responsibility, consistency between power and responsibility, both division and cooperation, and orderly operation, by taking into overall consideration the separation of complicated cases from simple ones and the specialization of adjudication, and both adjudication quality and efficiency are improved. By following the above ideas, Chaoyang District People's Court in Beijing has organized 26 fast-track sentencing teams for simple cases, each of which concludes over 650 cases annually, and 45 specialized judicial teams for trying the finance, intellectual property rights, real estate, bankruptcy and other complicated cases in a meticulous way, which have fairly tried a large number of major doubtful and complicated cases. Futian District People's Court in Shenzhen, Guangdong Province, has created a new mode of organizing judicial team as follows: in a fast-track sentencing, speedy proceeding and quick enforcement team, each judge is supported by multiple assistants; in an ordinary judicial team, there are 3 relatively fixed basic case-handling units, each of which consists of 1 judge and 2 assistants, so that the judicial team is both stable and flexible and the judicial resources allocation is optimized. In 2018, all kinds of judicial teams in Futian District People's Court concluded 107,301 cases, with a year to year increase of 16.32%, with the quality and efficiency of trial continuously being improved.

Reforming cases allocation mechanism. The courts at different levels have established a cases allocation mechanism where random allocation plays a major role and assignment a supporting role. Cases are randomly allocated to the judges based on the area and complexity of cases. If the judge handling a case has to be replaced due to challenge, or occupation mobility, physical condition, risk of corruption, and other reasons, the replacement is subject to review and approval by relevant court/tribunal president within its authorization, and the replacement result shall be notified to the litigants in a timely manner and made public on the working platform. The courts in Shanghai have formulated guidelines on random and automated allocation of cases and have realized random allocation of all civil and commercial cases. The Chengjiao People's Court in Sanya, Hainan Province has introduced an automated case allocation system, whereby, after scientifically presetting saturated workload of judges, cases are randomly allocated upon automated calculation of workload based on case-handling quota and unconcluded cases of each judge, and therefore address the problem of unbalanced allocation of cases through informatization.

Innovating the auxiliary trial work mode. The courts at different levels have formed work teams specializing in service of process, property preservation, seek and control for enforcement purpose, document uploading, online announcement and other affairs, being in charge of managing auxiliary trial affairs in a centralized way to improve work efficiency. The courts in Beijing, Shanghai, Jiangsu, Fujian, Guangdong, etc. actively explore the handling of notice service, material scanning, file filing and other auxiliary affairs by engaging social entities to provide services, to improve the efficiency of handling cases with external service providers. Shenzhen Intermediate People's Court in Guangdong Province has formulated the guidance documents on purchasing services from social entities, setting out the scope, procedures, and standards for courts to purchase services from social entities. Such guidance documents cover 41 services under seven categories, such as litigation service, adjudication and enforcement, court management, logistics support, judicial transparency, informatization, culture construction. In 2018, by outsourcing mediation assistance service, Shenzhen Intermediate People's Court successfully mediated 15,829 disputes before litigation; by using social services, it scanned hard-copy materials and generated soft- copies of more than 200,000 cases, constantly improving the efficiency of handling cases. Siming District People's Court and Lujiang Notary Public Office both in Xiamen, Fujian Province have created a litigation-notary collaborative innovation center, which is the first in China, clarifying that the notary offices may assist the people's courts with applicable procedural and auxiliary judicial works.

Improving the mechanism for regular handling of cases by court/ tribunal presidents. The courts nationwide have implemented the judge quota system. According to the requirements that registered judges must handle cases, the presidents (including vice presidents) of courts/tribunals at different levels generally engage in trial work upon being qualified as judge. In April 2017, the Supreme People's Court issued the *Guidelines on Promoting the handling of Cases by the Presidents of Courts/Tribunals at Different Levels*, establishing a mechanism for rigid constraint, evaluation and supervision on case-handling by court/tribunal presidents and improving the mechanism for court officials mainly responsible for adjudicating major doubtful and complicated cases, to give full play to the exemplary and leading role of court/tribunal presidents in handling cases. In 2018, in Jiangsu Province, the number of cases tried by court/tribunal presidents as handling judge or presiding judge accounted for 50.84% of the total number of cases in the province.

Improving the new trial management and supervision mechanism. In April 2017, the Supreme People's Court promulgated the *Opinions of the Supreme People's Court on Implementation of the Judicial Accountability System and Improvement of the Trial Supervision and Management Mechanism* to instruct the courts at different levels to improve the new supervision and management system. The courts at different levels have formulated a list of powers and responsibilities of court/tribunal presidents and related regulations to set out the scope and method for court/ tribunal presidents to exercise their power to supervise and manage the trials, and to actively build a supervision and management mechanism covering the entire court, all staff, and whole process through informatization. The court/ tribunal presidents may only express their opinions publicly on specific cases through professional judge conferences and the Judicial Committee, and such opinions shall be wholly recorded on the working platform, so that powers are delegated without indulgence and exercised under supervision. The courts in Jiangsu Province, Zhejiang Province, Shanghai, Sichuan Province and other regions, by relying on artificial intelligence and big data, explore how to achieve online supervision through automated recognition, labeling, system recommending, node control, authority freezing and other means. Tianjin Higher People's Court issued 29 categories of judicial standards in four batches covering adjudication process, power exercise, judicial transparency, litigation service and other areas. Chengdu Intermediate People's Court in Sichuan Province, by closely centering on five major links of case filing, adjudication, conclusion, appeal, and enforcement, and relying on online working platform, has achieved silent supervision on 183 work nodes and 68 monitoring nodes, in order to assist the judges in handling cases.

Improving the Presiding Judges' Conference system. Most of the courts at different levels have established the presiding judges' conference system to provide the judges with advice on correct application of law and provide opinions for reference by collegiate panels. In December 2018, the Supreme People's Court released the *Guiding Opinions on Improving the Working Mechanism for Presiding Judges' Conference of People's Courts* to improve the rules of procedure of professional judges' conference. Chongqing No. 2 Intermediate People's Court has established the systems of joint conference of judges in the tribunals and the cross- departmental conference of judges, with the number of cases submitted to the judicial committee for discussion being reduced by 42% year on year, thereby giving full play to the service and consultation functions of the conferences of judges and the function of filtration of the cases submitted to the judicial committee for discussion.

Reforming the system of judicial committee. The Supreme People's Court has formulated the guidelines to strengthen the function of the judicial committees in summarizing experience in adjudication, unifying the application of law and discussing and deciding on major issues in respect of adjudication. Except as otherwise provided by laws, the decisions made by the judicial committees on cases and the grounds therefor shall be made public in the written judgments. The people's courts above intermediate level shall hold criminal trials, civil-administrative trials and other professional committee conferences, based on professional background of and division of work among judicial committee members, as needed by adjudication. In addition to the cases required by the law and the major and complicated cases involving foreign affairs, security and social stability of the State, the judicial committees shall focus on the application of law in major, difficult and complicated cases. Since the launch of the reform, the number of cases submitted to the judicial committees in the people's courts at different levels for discussion has decreased significantly. In the Higher People's Court of the Inner Mongolia Autonomous Region, after the launch of the reform of judicial committee system, the number of judicial committee conferences held has reduced by 14.3% year on year, and the number of cases discussed has reduced by 45.1% year on year, and the function of the judicial committees has become more focused on summarizing experience in adjudication and discussing and deciding on major issues in respect of adjudication. In all courts in Hainan Province, after the launch of the reform of judicial committee system, the number of cases discussed by judicial committee has reduced by 41.75% year on year.

Establishing the system of guiding cases, the system of similar case search report, and the like. The Supreme People's Court has established the system of guiding cases and promulgated the detailed implementing rules for guiding cases. As of the end of 2018, a total of 106 guiding cases have been published in 20 batches. The cases tried by the courts at different levels that are similar to any guiding cases published by the Supreme People's

Court in terms of basic circumstances of the cases and governing laws shall be adjudicated by reference to the main reasons for the adjudication of such guiding cases and refer to such guiding cases in the statement of reasons for judgments. Most regions have established the system of reference cases, the system of guiding cases, and the like. Higher People's Court of Hainan Province has established a database of reference cases, so as to effectively reduce the phenomenon of "different judgments on similar cases". The courts in Hunan Province require handling judges to prepare related cases search reports in connection with the cases in dispute over law application or possibility of "different judgments on similar cases".

Improving the accountability system for illegal adjudication. The Supreme People's Court has formulated the relevant regulations, expressly providing that a judge shall be responsible for his/her performance of duties of adjudication, and for the quality of cases handled by him/her for life, and that a judge shall be held liable for illegal adjudication if he/she intentionally violates the laws in adjudication or commits any gross negligence resulting in any wrong judgment and causing any serious consequences; specifying the circumstances and conditions for exemption from responsibility for adjudication; on the principle that one who has powers shall assume corresponding responsibilities and one who is derelict in his duty shall be held liable, specifying the responsibility for supervision and management that a court/tribunal presidents shall assume if he/she improperly exercises any power of supervision and management over trials due to intentional or gross negligence; and improving the procedures for the determination, investigation, review and affixation of responsibility in respect of misjudged cases to strictly hold judges liable for illegal adjudication.

Establishing the system for punishing judges. In October 2016, the Supreme People's Court promulgated the opinions on the establishment of a system for punishing judges, which require the establishment of a system for punishing judges under which the people's courts and judge punishment committees assume their respective responsibilities. 27 provinces (autonomous regions, municipalities) have established judge punishment committees at the provincial level comprising judge representatives from the courts at the three levels and civilians, which shall be responsible for reviewing whether any judge has breached the responsibility for adjudication or committed any intentional or gross negligence or should assume the liability for illegal adjudication, and proposing punishments to be meted out, thus realizing both goals of imposing punishments in a timely manner according to law and ensuring job security.

Improving the judge performance evaluation system. The Supreme People's Court has promulgated the guidelines on improving the judge performance evaluation system and the performance-based bonus distribution mechanism, requiring that performance-based bonus may not be linked to judge's rank and shall be distributed mainly based on the level of responsibility, the quality, number, and difficulty of cases handled, and other factors and in favor of first-line handling judges. The courts at different levels shall formulate a judge performance evaluation system that is simple and easy to implement, by always combining objective quantification and subjective evaluation with a focus on quantitative evaluation, taking into full consideration of the differences between regions, trial levels, specialties and departments, in light of their respective local conditions.

Establishing the system of recording and notification and accountability investigation of leading officials and staff members of judicial organs for interventions in judicial activities and handling of specific case. The General Affairs Offices of the CCCPC and the State Council have jointly issued the *Regulations on the Recording, Notification, and Accountability Investigation of Leading Officials for Interventions in Judicial Activities and Handling of Specific Cases*. The Supreme People's Court has formulated the regulations on the recording and accountability investigation of leading officials and staff members of judicial organs for their intervention in case handling. The courts at different levels shall each establish a special database of interference with cases by external personnel and staff members in their case information management systems. The staff members of people's courts shall record in a complete, truthful and timely manner all the correspondences, letters and oral opinions relating to any specific cases passed on by various people not through the legal proceedings. Each people's court shall summarize and analyze the information in its database of intervention with cases by external personnel involving interference by officials on a quarterly basis, prepare a special report thereon and submit the same to the departments concerned and the people's court at the higher level. Any staff member of a people's court who fails to record such information or to record such information truthfully or any official in charge who incites any staff member not to record such information or not to record such information truthfully shall be subject to disciplinary actions depending on the actual circumstances. Since the establishment of the system, the intervention with judicial activities and handling of specific case has been significantly reduced, providing stronger institutional protection for the independent and fair exercise of adjudicative power by people's courts in accordance with the law.

Improving the mechanism for protecting judicial personnel in performing their duties in accordance with the law. In February 2017, the Supreme People's Court promulgated the implementation measures for protecting judges in performing their statutory duties in accordance with the law, which expressly provide that no administrative organ, social organization or individual may interfere with the adjudication of cases by judges in accordance with the law; no entity or individual may request any judge to do anything beyond the scope of his/her statutory duties; except for legal causes or according to legal procedures, no judge may be transferred to a different post, removed from office, dismissed, demoted or discharged or subject to any other punishment; any person who interferes with or obstructs any judicial activity, threatens, disturbs, takes revenge on, frames up, insults, defames or commits violence towards any judicial person or any close relative thereof shall be subject to serious punishment immediately in accordance with the law; and any person who insults or defames any judge by submitting any false report, lodging false accusations or fabricating false charges through the information network or otherwise shall be held legally liable under the law, so as to create a favorable institutional environment for judges to perform their duties.

III. Advancing the Reform of Organizational Structure of Courts

Improving an optimized, coordinated and efficient organizational system and functional system of the courts is an important part and goal of the judicial reform of the people's courts, and an important support for the modernization of adjudication system and adjudication capability. Since 2013, Chinese courts have actively promoted the reform of organizational system and internal organs of courts, optimized the jurisdiction and the allocation of powers and responsibilities, and promoted the combination of specialized adjudication and flat management, laying a solid foundation for serving the big picture, exercising judicial power in the interests of the People, and maintaining judicial fairness.

Setting up Circuit Courts of the Supreme People's Court. At the end of January 2015, the Supreme People's Court set up the First and Second Circuit Courts in Shenzhen and Shenyang respectively; at the end of December 2016, it set up the Third, Fourth, Fifth and Sixth Circuit Courts in Nanjing, Zhengzhou, Chongqing and Xi'an respectively. These Circuit Courts of the Supreme People's Court, as the standing local judicial organs dispatched by the Supreme People's Court, adjudicate the cases assigned by the Supreme People's Court according to law. The judgments and rulings made by these Circuit Courts have the equal effect as those made by the

Supreme People's Court. Since their establishment and as of the end of 2018, such six Circuit Courts have concluded 33,335 cases, accounting for 50.35% of the total number of the cases concluded by the Supreme People's Court, and have received a total of 117,090 visitors who brought complaints and appeals before them and resolved relevant disputes locally. By vigorously carrying out the circuit adjudication and actively innovating working mechanism, these Circuit Courts have effectively realized the shift of the work priority to the community level, made the People easy access to justice, improved work efficiency, effectively promoted social harmony and stability, and served and guaranteed the rule of law in respective circuits, thus being nicknamed by the People as the "Supreme People's Court at the doorstep", playing an important role in improving the socialist judicial system with Chinese characteristics and promoting the rule of law in a comprehensive manner.

Enhancing the construction of a specialized IP adjudication system. In order to further enhance the judicial protection of intellectual property rights (IP) and unifying the adjudicative criteria for IP cases, with the approval by the Standing Committee of the National People's Congress, IP courts were established in Beijing, Guangzhou and Shanghai on November 6, December 16 and December 28, 2014 respectively. The Supreme People's Court has promulgated relevant judicial interpretations, defining the jurisdiction of IP courts over the cases, and providing guidelines on the appointment of IP judges, participation in litigious activities by technological investigation officers of IP courts and other issues. The IP courts have built a new image of judicial protection of IP in China through fair adjudication of typical cases, timely publication of typical cases and otherwise. As of the end of 2018, these three IP courts had accepted a total of 90,578 cases and concluded 74,007 cases. In addition, the Supreme People's Court has also promoted the establishment of 19 IP courts in 16 provinces and cities such as Jiangsu Province, in order to realize centralized jurisdiction over some IP cases across regions. On January 1, 2019, the IP Tribunal of the Supreme People's Court, which was established according to the decision of the Standing Committee of the National People's Congress, was officially opened to make unified adjudication of highly professional and technical civil and administrative appeals, such as those involving patent, to form a national mechanism for adjudicating IP appeals. The above-mentioned reform measures have effectively promoted the specialized adjudication of, centralized jurisdiction over, and intensified procedures for IP cases, and improved the IP adjudication system with Chinese characteristics.

Launching pilot reform of trans-regional courts in Beijing and Shanghai. In order to ensure lawful and fair adjudication of trans-regional cases, the Beijing the Fourth Intermediate People's Court and the Shanghai the Third Intermediate People's Court were established in Beijing and Shanghai respectively in December 2014, as the pilot trans-regional people's courts, through which experience has been accumulated in exploring how to establish a new pattern of litigation system in which general cases are adjudicated at local courts and special cases are adjudicated at trans-regional courts. These two courts are responsible for adjudicating major civil, commercial, administrative, environmental and resource protection, food and drug safety and certain criminal cases involving different administrative regions, to ensure fair adjudication of cases involving local interests. From 2015 to 2018, the number of first-instance administrative cases brought against a district/county government and subject to the centralized jurisdiction of and accepted by the Beijing the Fourth Intermediate People's Court increased by 650%. As appointed by the Supreme People's Court, from October 26, 2017, this court began to accept the appeals of environmental-protection administrative cases adjudicated by relevant courts in Tianjin, marking an important step in cross-provincial jurisdiction of cases. The number of administrative cases accepted by the Shanghai the Third Intermediate People's Court increases by over 30% per year. In 2018, the number of settled and dropped administrative cases before this court increased by 126.67% over the previous year. These two trans-regional courts have fairly adjudicated a series of cases with major social impacts, effectively addressing the issue of "at home v. away in litigation" and enhancing the public credibility of the judiciary.

Setting up Shanghai Financial Court. According to the decision of the Standing Committee of the National People's Congress, Shanghai Financial Court was formally established on August 20, 2018 with special jurisdiction over the finance-related civil-commercial cases and finance-related administrative cases subject to the jurisdiction of an Intermediate People's Court. The Supreme People's Court has promulgated several judicial interpretations, clarifying the specific jurisdiction of the Shanghai Financial

Court. As of the end of 2018, Shanghai Financial Court had accepted 1,897 cases, with a total value of object of RMB 25.2 billion, mainly involving disputes related to liability for misrepresentation in a securities trading, financial loan contracts, corporate bond trading, repurchase of pledged securities, financial leasing contracts, for-profit trust, etc.

Setting up Internet courts in Hangzhou, Beijing and Guangzhou. Internet court is a major institutional innovation whereby Chinese courts actively address the judicial needs in the Internet era and implement the "Internet Power" strategy. Hangzhou Internet Court, Beijing Internet Court and Guangzhou Internet Court were successively established on August 18, 2017, September 9, 2018 and September 28, 2018. In September 2018, the Supreme People's Court promulgated several judicial interpretations on trial of cases by the Internet courts, clarifying the jurisdiction, appeal mechanism, online litigation rules, and requirements for construction of litigation platform of Internet courts. Internet courts have actively promoted the principle of "online disputes to be tried online" and facilitated the online verification of litigant's identity, online collection of evidentiary materials, online service of legal instruments, etc., thus significantly improving judicial efficiency. In Hangzhou Internet Court, the online case-filing rate has reached 89.2%, the online court-session rate has reached 59.9%, the online case-concluding rate has reached 83.6%, the duration of an online court session is 28 minutes on average, and the trial period is 41 days on average, saving 60% and 50% of the time respectively compared with the traditional trial mode. With an emphasis on summarizing and refining the rules for adjudicating Internet-related cases, the Internet courts have successfully and efficiently adjudicated a number of difficult and complicated Internet-related cases of new types, including the ownership of big data, the liability for contracting fault in online shopping, and the ownership of copyright in AI works, thus strongly promoting the rule of law in cyberspace governance.

Reforming the organizational system of military courts. Military courts are the judicial organs set up by the State in the army. According to the overall arrangement by the Central Government, the basis for the setup of military courts was changed from branches of services and systems into combat zones. After the said reform, the new organizational system of military courts includes the PLA Military Court (at the level of higher court), the Military Court of the East Combat Zone of the PLA, the Military Court of the South Combat Zone of the PLA, the First and Second Military Courts of the West Combat Zone of the PLA, the Military Court of the Northern Combat Zone of the PLA, the Military Court of the Central Combat Zone of the PLA and the Military Court Directly under the Headquarters of the PLA (at the level of intermediate court), and 26 military courts of the PLA in Shanghai, Nanjing, and Hangzhou and other cities (at the level of grassroots court).

Promoting the reform of internal organs of people's courts below the provincial level. The Supreme People's Court, in conjunction with the related departments of the Central Government, has actively promoted the reform of internal organs of people's courts below the provincial level. In line with the principle of coordination, optimization and efficiency, the structure of people's courts shall be streamlined, the number of internal organs shall be strictly limited, the adjudicating departments shall be scientifically set up, and non-adjudicating departments with overlapping functions and similar services shall be integrated, in order to promote flat management. As of the end of 2018, Tianjin and Shanghai had completed the reform of the internal organs. The number of internal organs of the intermediate and grassroots people's courts in Tianjin has been reduced from 361 to 234, with a reduction of 35.2%; the number of internal organs (excluding detached tribunals) of 17 grassroots courts in Shanghai has been reduced from 298 to 197, with a reduction of 33.9%. For the reform of internal organs of the grassroots courts in other provinces (autonomous regions and municipalities), relevant plan is going through reviewing, approving and filing procedure.

IV. Strengthening the System and Mechanism of Judicial Protection of Human Rights

To respect and protect human rights is an important principle set forth in the *Constitution of the People's Republic of China*, and also an important content of the socialist judicial system with Chinese characteristics. Chinese courts have achieved positive results in the development of the mechanism of judicial protection of human rights through pushing forward the reform of trial-centered criminal litigation system, strictly adhering to the principles of legality, evidence judgment and presumption of innocence, resolutely preventing wrongful convictions and protecting the lawyers' right to practice according to law.

Pushing forward the reform of trial-centered criminal litigation system. The Supreme People's Court, in conjunction with the Supreme People's Procuratorate, the Ministry of Public Security, the Ministry of State Security and the Ministry of Justice, promulgated several guiding opinions on pushing forward the reform of trial-centered criminal litigation system and regulations on strictly excluding illegally obtained evidences in handling of criminal cases. The reform of the trial-centered criminal litigation system implements the principles of evidence judgment, strictly excluded illegally obtained evidences and presumption of innocence, and requires strengthening the substantiation of court trials, improving the mechanism for supervising investigation and prosecution activities through trials, preventing forced confessions, collection of evidence through illegal means and other illegal acts from the source, and promoting the formation of a criminal litigation pattern with trial-centered litigation, hearing-centered court trial, and evidence-centered court trial, so that the facts of cases found during the investigations, prosecutions and trials will be proved to be true according to law. The Supreme People's Court implemented on a pilot basis the following procedures for pretrial conferences, excluding illegally obtained evidences and conducting court investigation under ordinary procedure in first instance trial in handling criminal cases in 18 intermediate people's courts across the country in June 2017 and required the tentative implementation in all courts nationwide on and from January 1, 2018. All regions have fully implemented the principle of evidence judgment, solidly promoted the substantiation of court trials, and improved the system for summoning key witnesses, appraisers and investigators to testify before courts, so as to give fullest play to the role of witnesses', investigators', and appraisers' testifying before courts and effectively resolve the disputes between the prosecutors and the defenders. In 2017, the courts in Guangdong Province accepted 1,582 applications for excluding illegally obtained evidences, initiated the process of excluding illegally obtained evidences for 1,424 times, and excluded 235 pieces of illegally obtained evidences, which is more than the sum of the evidences being excluded in the previous three years. Intermediate People's Court of Chengdu in Sichuan Province took the lead in carrying out the reform of substantiation of court trials nationwide, by fully implementing the provisions regarding holding pretrial conferences, strictly excluding illegally obtained evidence, summoning key witnesses to testify before court, admitting evidence in court, pronouncing judgment in court, trying all cases with lawyer's defense, preparing complicated written judgments or simple ones as the case may be, opening exemplary court trials, etc., so as to ensure that court trials play a decisive role in finding the facts, admitting evidences, protecting the right of appeal and making judgments fairly. In these exemplary court trials, a total of 1,469 witnesses, including 818 general witnesses, 114 appraisers, 455 investigators, 17 experts, and 65 victims, testified before courts. Intermediate People's Court of Wenzhou in Zhejiang Province has improved the mechanism for protecting personnel testifying before court, issued the detailed rules on investigators' appearance in court as witnesses, provided remote rooms for offering testimonies, devices for concealing faces of the witnesses and other appropriate facilities, established the mechanism for protecting the rights and interests of the witnesses in conjunction with the public security and procuratorial organs, and formulated the standard of the subsidies for witnesses testifying in court. Since 2015, the courts in Wenzhou have given notices to require 1,434 people in 915 criminal cases to appear in courts, and 915 people in 581 criminal cases have actually appeared in courts to testify, with the rate of testimony in courts being 63.8%.

Preventing and correcting wrongful convictions. The Supreme People's Court promulgated the guidelines on improving a working mechanism preventing unjust, false and erroneous criminal cases, providing that the defendants should be acquitted for lack of evidence and no one should be prosecuted without criminal evidence, rather than imposing a relatively light penalty or otherwise imposing penalty on the defendant by leaving some leeway. On December 2, 2016, the Second Circuit Court of the Supreme People's Court publicly pronounced the judgment on the case of Nie Shubin suspected of intentional homicide and raping women, overruling the judgment made by the lower court and pronouncing Nie Shubin innocent, thereby correcting the judgment on this major doubtful and complicated case that had lasting for 22 years, and reflecting great importance attached by the people's courts to judicial protection of human rights and seriously observe the legal principles, such as evidence judgment and presumption of innocence. Since 2013, the people's courts have corrected the judgments on 46 major unjust, false and erroneous criminal cases involving 94 people, including Nie Shubin case, Hugjiltu case and Zhang Hui and Zhang Gaoping (nephew and uncle) case, thereby greatly enhancing the public's confidence in judicial impartiality. From 2014 to 2018, the people's courts at different levels pronounced 4,868 defendants innocent as per law, ensuring that the innocent will not be prosecuted under law.

Improving the fast-track sentencing procedure for criminal cases and the system of imposing lenient punishments on those confessing to their crimes and accepting punishments. With the authorization of the Standing Committee of the National People's Congress, since August 26, 2014, China has launched a two-year pilot reform on fast-track sentencing procedure for criminal cases in 217 grassroots courts in Beijing and other 17 cities. During the period of the pilot reform, the pilot courts tried and concluded 52,540 criminal cases using the fast-track sentencing procedure, involving 54,572 defendants in total, accounting for 35.88% of criminal cases in which not more than one-year sentences were pronounced by such pilot courts in the same period, and 18.48% of the criminal cases tried by such pilot courts in the same period; among such cases, 92.35% were concluded within 10 days, 65.04% higher than those subject to the summary procedure, and the pronouncement rate in court is 96.05%, 41.22% higher than those subject to the summary procedure. Haidian District People's Court in Beijing has explored the mode of whole-course fast-track sentencing procedure to effectively reduce the time of circulation of cases at all the stages. Under the said mode, the average duration of the judicial procedure in which the defendants were under detention was 33 days, about 70% shorter than that of the similar cases concluded using the summary procedure prior to the reform. Among all the cases subject to the fast-track sentencing procedure, the appeal rate of the plaintiffs with incidental civil action was 0, and that of defendants was 2.01%, the appeal rate of procuratorial organs was only 0.01%, 9.52% lower than that of all criminal cases. According to a third party assessment conducted by the China University of Political Science and Law, the defendants' satisfaction rate with the effect of the fast-track sentencing procedure reached 97.69%. Through shortening pre-trial detention and imposing sentences on the defendants quickly and leniently, the fast-track sentencing procedure can give full play to the function of social correction, and help the offenders reform themselves and return to the society. In September 2016, the 22nd Session of the Standing Committee of the 12th National People's Congress reviewed a report on the pilot reform, fully affirmed the efforts in these pilot reforms, and decided to incorporate the pilot reform of fast-track sentencing procedure for criminal cases into the reform of the system of imposing lenient punishments on those confessing to their crimes and accepting punishments and to continue the pilot reform. During the period between September 2016 and September 2018, 281 pilot courts were identified, and 205,510 criminal cases were concluded by applying the system of imposing lenient punishments on those confessing to their crimes and accepting punishments, accounting for 53.5% of the criminal cases concluded by the pilot courts during this period. On October 26, 2018, at the 6th Session of the Standing Committee of the 13th National People's Congress, a decision was made on amending the *Criminal Procedure Law of the People's Republic of China* to incorporate the achievements made in the pilot reform of imposing lenient punishments on those confessing to their crimes and accepting punishments into the latest amended Criminal Procedure Law and promote them nationwide.

Deepening the reform on standardization of sentencing. At the end of 2013, the Supreme People's Court promulgated the *Guiding Opinions on Sentencing by the People's Courts*, to regulate the judges' discretion in sentencing, set up an independent debate procedure regarding sentencing, and promote the standardization of sentencing throughout the country. In 2016, the Supreme People's Court designated certain courts to further extended the kinds of crimes, by incorporating dangerous driving and other seven crimes under the governance of the above opinion, as well as the kinds of punishments, from imprisonment and criminal detention to fines and probation, and ensure the standardization of sentencing, suiting punishment to crime. Through the implementation of the reform, the methodology in sentencing has become more standardized and scientific, and the sentences received have become fairer and more balanced, bringing about a procedure with more transparency and fairness.

Strictly standardizing commutation of punishment, parole and temporary enforcement of sentences outside prison. In April 2014, the Supreme People's Court promulgated several judicial interpretations regarding the adjudication procedures for commutation of punishment and parole, requiring the establishment of the system of public adjudication on commutation of punishment and parole and the system of periodic publication of typical cases. In 2015, a national information website on the cases of commutation of punishment, parole and temporary enforcement of sentences outside prison granted by the courts went live, to publicize the information of the whole process from case filing to judgment entering of the cases involving commutation of punishment and parole, so that commutation of punishment and parole is conducted under the supervision of the public. In November 2016, the Supreme People's Court promulgated the *Provisions on the Specific Application of the Law to Handling Commutation and Parole Cases*, to further clarify the nature and application of commutation of punishment and parole, and unify the criteria of deciding such cases, ensuring that fairness and equality are well addressed therein. In November 2017, the Supreme People's Court launched a national online platform for processing cases involving commutation of punishment and parole. The new platform promotes the case information sharing and online case-handling collaboration among the people's courts and people's procuratorates and the penalty execution authorities and between the people's courts at different levels, ensuring the whole process of adjudicating cases involving commutation of punishment and parole traceable and under supervision.

Amending and improving the court rules. In February 2015, the Supreme People's Court and the Ministry of Public Security jointly promulgated a circular, providing that when appearing in the court, the criminal defendants and appellants are no longer required to wear their clothing bearing the name of the detention houses and the criminals in jail are no longer required to wear their prison uniforms, and that when a people's court brings a criminal defendant or appellant under detention to trial, the detention house shall turn over the criminal defendant or appellant in formal or informal wear to the people's court to reflect modern judicial civilization. On April 13, 2016, the Supreme People's Court promulgated the *Court Rules of People's Courts of the People's Republic of China* as mended latest, further specifying the code of conduct in tribunals, in order to maintain the order of tribunals , strengthen judicial protection of human rights, and make the tribunals be more open, convenient, civilized and safer and become venues where the people can experience fairness and justice.

Improving the mechanism for protecting lawyers' rights in practice in accordance with the law. In December 2015, the Supreme People's Court promulgated several opinions on protecting lawyers' rights in practice, requiring protection of lawyers' rights to know, access to case files, obtain evidence, debate in court and their rights of representation, application for excluding illegal obtained evidence and for appeal, and providing protection and convenience to lawyers in performing their duties under the law. The mechanism of soliciting lawyers' opinions in the review of death sentence has been established, which require protection of lawyers' rights, including the right to access to case filing information and case files, and provide that lawyers can directly make defenses to the judges of the Supreme People's Court, so as to ensure the fairness of review of death sentence. In October 2017, the Supreme People's Court and the Ministry of Justice promulgated the *Measures on the Pilot Work to Apply Lawyer Defense to All Criminal Cases* and launched the pilot in Shanghai and Zhejiang Province. On December 30, 2015, the Supreme People's Court opened the lawyer service platform, on which the lawyers can, among other things, file cases, access to case fillies and contact judges on online. As of the end of 2018, 1,924 courts nationwide have opened a lawyer service platform, providing services to lawyers for a total of 1.27 million times. The lawyer service platform of the Supreme People's Court has provided 22,067 law firms and 89,338 lawyers with online services such as case filing, access to case files, case inquiry, payment, refund, electronic service, and contact with judges. In 2018, the total number of visits to the lawyer service platform was 43,527, which quadrupled the sum of the year 2017. Zhejiang Province has established a lawyer service centers in the courts at three levels, to provide access to case information and files, meeting with judges, rest, dressing and other services, and explored in establishing certain special facilities at law firms for handling lawsuit-related matters on line.

Improving the system of state compensation. The Supreme People's Court has formulated the *Interpretation on Several Issues Concerning the Application of Law in the Handling of Criminal Cases Regarding Compensation*, improved the cross-examination procedure for compensation cases, standardized the measurement of compensation for moral damages, and expressed opinions on further improving state compensation in *wrongful convictions* , so as to give full play of the function of remedy of state compensation. From 2014 to 2018, the people's courts at different levels accepted 31,434 cases of state compensation. The victims suffered *wrongful convictions* or their close relatives such as Hugjiltu case, Zhang Hui and Zhang Gaoping case, Nie Shubin case and Liu Zhonglin case, have received the compensations in a timely manner according to law. For example, Liu Zhonglin has received a state compensation of RMB 4.6 million from the Intermediate People's Court of Liaoyuan in Jilin Province, the authority liable for compensation.

Improving the judicial aid system. In July 2016, the Supreme People's Court promulgated the Opinions on Strengthening and Standardizing the Work of National Judicial Aid Conducted by the People's Courts, providing uniform regulations for acceptance and handling of cases, scope of aid, procedure of aid, standard of aid, fund guarantee and appropriation of funds, to realize the administration of the aid system by law and the handling of aid cases according to judicial procedures. On September 18, 2016, the Supreme People's Court set up the judicial aid committee, and the local people's courts at different levels also set up their judicial aid committees. In conducting the work of judicial aid, the courts in Tianjin have strengthened the joint actions with the aid provided by other judicial authorities, social organizations and other provinces and cities, to realize seamless connection between the judicial aid and social security, and improve the accuracy, coverage and timeliness of judicial aid. The courts in Sichuan Province have developed simplified judicial aid application process and an online judicial aid platform, to realize online and standardized handling of cases of judicial aid.

Standardizing the judicial procedure for handling the properties involved in cases. In October 2014, the Supreme People's Court promulgated several judicial interpretations regarding the enforcement of property involved in criminal judgments, to standardize the enforcement procedure of handling the properties involved in criminal cases, including confiscation and recovery of properties, measures of realization, handling of disputes in enforcement, etc. Between 2015 and 2018, the Supreme People's Court has, in conjunction with the related authorities of the Central Government, constantly pushed forward the establishment of inter-departmental information platforms for centralized management of properties involved in cases, improved the procedures of advance disposal and pretrial return of properties, defined the interested parties' right of action, and improved the remedy mechanism and the accountability system. In May 2015, the first inter-departmental center for the management of properties involved in criminal lawsuits in our country was established in Zhuji, Zhejiang Province. The center established a centralized information platform for the management of properties involved in cases. All the public security, procuratorial and judicial departments are required to enter the information about the properties involved in cases under their respective management into the platform, thereby realizing electronic handover of properties involved in cases, facilitating the handling of cases and standardizing the procedures for handling properties involved in cases.

V. Promoting People's Access to and Benefits from the Judiciary

Exercising judicial power in the interests of the People and administrating the justice impartially is taken as the underpinning of the people's courts. The people's courts have been reforming the system of acceptance and handling of cases, strengthening the establishment of litigation service centers and people's tribunals, improving the multiple disputes resolution mechanism and the mechanism of separating complicated cases from simple ones, promoting reforms on family law trials and taking other measures, to constantly enhance the exercise of judicial power in the interests of the People and make the People have a stronger sense of gain in the judicial reform.

Comprehensively implementing the case filing registration system. Since May 1, 2015, the people's courts have reformed the case filing system by introducing the case filing registration system and eliminating the prior examination. This new system requires each case meeting the acceptance conditions shall be placed on file and be accepted and handled, thereby effectively protecting the litigants' right to file a lawsuit and completely eliminating the institutional barriers causing the difficulties in case filing. As of the end of 2018, the courts nationwide registered over 64.89 million cases, with an on-the-spot case registration rate of over 95%.

The courts nationwide have simplified the case filing procedure and by means of notification of case filing, once-and-for-all list of supplements and corrections, request for response within prescribed time limit and otherwise, ensured the successful filing of cases by the litigants in one attempt. The courts in Beijing introduced a mechanism of supervision and complaints rapid-handling over case filing, which enables the courts to promptly respond to and resolve litigants' complaints and problems therein. In 2016 alone, this mechanism successfully resolves complaints lodged by more than 1,300 times, thereby ensuring the effective implementation of the case filing registration system. The implementation of this reform has been under stronger monitoring by the Supreme People's Court. The practices such as setting additional conditions to constrain case filing have been firmly forbidden in order to prevent the targeted difficulties in case filing from rebounding.

Diversifying the case filing routines. Relying on information technologies, the people's courts have been promoting a variety of convenient methods of filing cases, forming a new pattern of case filing with local case filing as main method, with online case filing, self-service case filing, cross-regional case filing, collaborative case filing and so forth as supplementary methods. The People now can file a lawsuit more conveniently and quicker, and the efficiency of case filing has improved significantly. The courts in all regions have actively promoted online case filing while actively improving conventional channels for case filing such as on the spot of the courthouse, through appointment, and on site. Some courts actively explore cross-regional case filing service, enabling the litigants to file a lawsuit in a nearby court or any court chosen by them, and reducing the burdens of litigants supposed to travel. As of the end of 2018, 3,044 courts nationwide had introduced online case filing service, and 2.38 million cases had been filed online; 1,154 courts had provided cross-regional case filing service, and 120,000 cases had been filed via the cross-regional filing system ; 1,863 courts had set up self-service case filing areas, and the litigants or lawyers had filed 1.03 million cases by themselves. 7 courts in Beijing, Tianjin and Hebei have established a new mode of collaborative case filing mechanism, which allows the litigants equal access to the inclusive, convenient and efficient case filing services provided irrespective of whereabouts. The People's Court of Pudong New Area, Shanghai has developed a "QR code" self- service case filing system, through which each case may be filed within 15 minutes on average.

Enhancing modernization of litigation services. In December 2014, the Supreme People's Court promulgated the several guiding opinions on promoting the establishment of litigation service centers at people's courts. As of the end of 2018, 98% of the courts nationwide had established litigation service halls, with up to 1.82 million square meters in area, 2,995 courts had launched the litigation service websites, 1,623 courts had launched online litigation service APPs, and 2,813 courts had set up 12368 litigation service hotline. The courts at all different levels have been actively and creatively developing online platforms such as 24-hour self-service courts, online mediation rooms, digital case files access services, online video systems for complaints and appeals, and have been equipped with Intelligent Visitors Management Systems, Court-Operated Robotic Assistant, litigation assistance machines, litigation risk assessment machines, convenient self-service terminals, intelligent cloud cabinets, smart navigation and others alike. The online services provided through various platforms include case filing, payment , mediation, access to information, submission of documents, examination of case files, electronic service of legal process, contact with judges, etc., amounting to 48 functions which is 40 more than available services in 2009. Along with the mechanism of separating complicated cases from simple ones, a combined mode of "cases identification + mediation + fast track sentencing+ speedy proceeding" has been developed in the litigation service centers. Such mode well functions with staffs in charge of cases identification, venues specialized for mediation, equipped open tribunals for fast–track sentencing procedures, optimized litigation-mediation coordination mechanism, plenty of judges and clerks specialized in fast-track and speedy proceedings, and an underlying electronic system. Owing to this mode, the litigation service centers have been transformed into one-stop hubs resolving a majority of cases filed in grassroots courts fully exerting their roles as legal "clinics" of disputes resolution. Most courts nationwide have been carrying out reforms into this new mode, 2,464 courts have appointed 14,669 cases identification clerks, and 12,234 full-time mediators have been recruited. As of the end of 2018, the courts nationwide had resolved 1.71 million cases through the multiple disputes resolution mechanism without proceeding into trial, 1.2 million cases through mediation after case filing, and 1.75 million cases through fast-track sentencing procedures and speedy proceedings in litigation service centers. The courts in Anhui Province have established family affairs, labor, property and other dispute mediation divisions at their litigation service centers, as well as the workstations consisting of the representatives of the Party Congress and People's Congress and the member of People's Political Consultative Conference, lawyer's offices and people's mediation rooms, and carried out online and remote mediations, multiple disputes resolution, achieving remarkable success. The courts in Zhejiang Province have been carrying out the 'at most one visit' scheme, and have successfully alleviated citizens' litigation costs and burden by promoting services both online and offline. The courts in Tibet, Ningxia and other regions have set up circuiting courts in vehicles to provide easier access to justice for the litigants.

Improving the multiple dispute resolution mechanisms. The multiple dispute resolution mechanism is a significant component of China's efforts in modernizing governance. In June 2016, the Supreme People's Court promulgated the *Opinions on Further Deepening the Reform of Multiple Dispute Resolution Mechanisms in People's Courts*, proposing a "three-step strategy", namely "the State firstly develops strategies for developments, then the judiciary provides legal safeguards, and finally advances relative legislative proceedings". Modernized conception of disputes resolution has been established as "State-led, judiciary-advanced, society participatory, multiple routines, and safeguarded by rule of law". The Supreme People's Court has, in conjunction with the Ministry of Public Security, the Ministry of Justice, the Ministry of Human Resources and

Social Security, the Ministry of Civil Affairs, the National Development and Reform Commission, the China Securities Regulatory Commission, the China Insurance Regulatory Commission, the All-China Federation of Returned Overseas Chinese, the National Federation of Industry and Commerce, the All-China Women's Federation, and other authorities respectively, issued over 20 documents in respect of the litigation-mediation coordination mechanism, covering issues related to people's mediation, family law disputes, securities and futures disputes, insurance disputes, and assigning auxiliary judicial affairs to notary offices. A solid framework of multiple disputes resolution mechanisms has been establishing. The Supreme People's Court has promulgated the *Provisions on Mediation Services Specially Invited by People's Courts* to instruct all regions to enhance litigation-mediation coordination and promote timely and efficient resolution of contradictions and disputes. As of the end of 2018, the courts nationwide had established 3,320 litigation-mediation coordination centers, and recruited nearly 22,194 specially invited mediation organizations and 78,153 specially invited mediators, which had mediated 1,862,800 cases as assigned or entrusted by the courts. The people's courts at different levels have established litigation- mediation coordination platforms in various forms, which have operated in a standard manner and exercised the functions of cases identification, designated mediation before and after case-filing, after-case filing designated mediation and judicial confirmation, etc., and improved the mechanism of connection between the courts and administrative agencies, people's mediation organizations, business-oriented mediation association, commercial mediation organizations, arbitration institutions and notary offices. As of the end of December 2018, by innovatively combining "Internet and dispute resolution" and establishing unified online mediation platforms, 1,258 courts had conducted online mediation and thereby resolved 11,394 disputes. In 2018, the courts in Beijing referred 304,000 first-instance civil cases to the "multiple routines of mediation + fast-track" mechanism, and successfully concluded 176,000 cases via this mechanism, accounting for 39% of the first-instance civil cases concluded that year. The courts in Zhejiang have established an "online platform for diversified resolution of contradictions and disputes" and formed a progressive and funnel-typed mechanism of filtering and resolving contradictions and disputes level by level. As of the end of November 2018, the platform had attracted 432,000 registered users and 34,000 registered mediators, received over 240,000 applications for mediation, and successfully mediated 208,000 cases, with a success rate of 88.17%. The courts in Zhejiang Province upgraded the disputes resolution mechanism from "resolving small dispute before it goes out the village" to "resolving dispute before it goes out the house" by inheriting "Maple Bridge Experience" and innovating based on it. Intermediate People's Court of Ma'anshan in Anhui Province has promoted the diversification reform further by conducting online mediation off site and remotely, achieving success in 95.1% online mediations. Intermediate People's Court of Meishan in Sichuan Province has fully mobilized and utilized various kinds of resources for dispute resolution, and solved 80.72% of controversies and disputes by means of alternative dispute resolution between 2014 and 2016, with only 7.06% of cases entering into the judicial procedures to be adjudicated, thereby creating the "Meishan Experience" connecting the litigation and alternative dispute resolution. Heilongjiang Province, Anhui Province, Fujian Province, Shandong Province and Xiamen City in Fujian Province have promulgated several local regulations on diversified resolution of contradictions and disputes, providing legal protection for dispute resolution and social governance.

Establishing and improving the lawyer mediation system. In September 2017, the Supreme People's Court and the Ministry of Justice jointly promulgated the *Opinions on the Pilot Program of Lawyer Mediation*, and launched the pilot program in 11 provinces (or municipalities) such as Beijing, Heilongjiang Province and Shanghai. For more than one year after the launch, the pilot courts established 657 lawyer mediation rooms, and included 1,290 lawyer mediation organizations and 12,360 lawyer mediators in their panel of specially appointed mediation organizations and mediators; these lawyers participated in the mediation of 54,898 cases and successfully mediated 25,569 cases; they made 8,529 applications for judicial confirmation, issued 824 payment orders, and made 3,325 applications for enforcement of mediation agreement, effectively exploiting their advantages and playing their role in dispute resolution. 63% of the courts nationwide have established a system for lawyers to lodge appeals on behalf of their clients, and 78% of the courts nationwide have established a system for lawyers to reside in courts. As of the end of 2018, the lawyers residing in the courts nationwide have accepted 791,932 cases, lodged 26,942 appeals on behalf of their clients, and participated in the resolution of 27,499 disputes.

Pushing forward the reform of the mechanism of identifying complicated cases from simple cases. In September 2016, the Supreme People's Court promulgated the *Opinions on Furthering Separation of Complicated Cases from Simple Cases and Optimizing the Allocation of Judicial Resources*. In May 2017, the Supreme People's Court promulgated the *Operating Rules for Separating Complicated Civil-commercial Cases from Simple Ones and Resort to Mediation and Fast Track*, to instruct the courts at different levels to optimize the allocation of judicial resources, to innovate and improve the working mechanism, and to alleviate the caseloads. The Supreme People's Court has formulated the criterion of model courts for piloting in identifying complicated cases from simple cases and designated 80 such courts. In 2018, the number of cases concluded according to summary procedures increased by 38.81% compared with 2014. Courts nationwide have actively carried out creative mechanisms such as court trial focusing on essential factors, writ, and exemplary litigation to deepen the reform and address the new problem of rapid increase in the number of cases, shorten the case-handling period, and improve judicial efficiency. Most grassroots courts in Jiangsu have established divisions for fast-track sentencing of small claim cases, each of which comprises one judge and one clerk, adopts the mode of trail focusing on essential factors, simplifies the written judgments, announces judgments ex tempore in principle, and concludes a case within 20 days on average, with nearly 70% of cases dropped after mediation. Intermediate People's Court of Shenyang in Liaoning Province has actively implemented the system of pre-trial conference to handle procedural issues, such as notification of rights and obligations, petition for excusing judges, clarification the respective arguments of the plaintiffs and defendants, ascertaining non-disputed facts, identification of the points at issue, and urging the parties involved to submit evidences related to such points at issue. Since the launch of the reform, the duration of court trial has been reduced by about 50 minutes on average.

Deepening the reform of the system of handling letters and visits involving lawsuits. The Supreme People's Court has been actively promoting the handling of letters and visits involving lawsuits in accordance with the law. The courts at different levels have been improving the working mechanism of separating litigation from letters and visits and solving the people's lawful and reasonable claims with earnest efforts. The Supreme People's Court has established an online platform for handling letters and visits, enabling the litigants to check anytime anywhere about the progress and feedback after filing the information about their complaints and submitting, which further unblocks the complaint channels and alleviates people's burden. The Supreme People's Court has launched an online video system to receive complaints, which is connected with the courts at four levels nationwide, enabling the Supreme People's Court, local people's courts and complainants to communicate face-to-face remotely, which reduces the visits to Beijing by about 30%. The Supreme People's Court has preliminarily established a national platform for courts to handle letters and visits involving lawsuits, to gather relevant information on the nationwide scale, and functions well in respects of publication and submission of the information of letters and visits, supervision of the handling of letters and visits, and realized quick and accurate communication between the lower and upper courts consequently, which improves the efficiency, as well as unified the coordination mechanism.

Pushing forward the reform of the approaches and working mechanisms for family law cases. In April 2016, the Supreme People's Court promulgated the *Guiding Opinions on Carrying out the Pilot Reform of the Approach and Working Mechanism for Family Law Cases*, exploring the ways to solve family disputes in a professional, socialized and people-oriented manner, and actively pushing forward the pilot reform. The pilot courts have made efforts in establishing family divisions or collegial panels for family law disputes, introducing domestic disputes investigators, social workers, child psychologists and others alike to provide mental guidance and other expertise to the parties involved, and advancing the integration of judicial, administrative and social resources, which constitutes a new mechanism for comprehensively solving family law disputes. On July 19, 2017, the Supreme People's Court took the lead in establishing a joint meeting mechanism involving 15 authorities for advancing this reform. On July 18, 2018, the Supreme People's Court promulgated the *Opinions on Further Deepening the Reform of the Approach and Working Mechanism for Family Law Cases*. The courts in Hebei, Shandong, Zhejiang, Fujian, Shaanxi, Qinghai, Gansu, Tibet and other provinces and regions have established similar joint meeting mechanisms, contributing to the establishment of a working pattern where party committees exercise leadership, local governments fulfill their duties, courts lead, and the public participates. The higher people's courts in Liaoning, Inner Mongolia, Anhui, Ningxia, Guangxi and other provinces and regions have formulated comprehensive procedures for trials in regard to family law cases. The courts in Chongqing, Qinghai and other provinces and regions have strengthened the psychological assessment and intervention in handling cases, effectively preventing civil cases from deteriorating into criminal cases; Putuo District People's Court in Shanghai has created the mechanism of "representative of children's interests" where the staff at the Office of National Working Committee on Women and Children act as representatives to effectively protect the legitimate rights and interests of juveniles through independent investigations, evidence collection and participation in court trials; Intermediate People's Court of Linfen in Shanxi has been exploring a mechanism of revisiting the parties and provides supports, so that the humanistic care from the socialist judiciary could be felt. Xicheng District People's Court in Beijing and Yiling District People's Court in Yichang, Hubei have been actively trying a cooling-off period in marriage mechanism in divorce cases.

Pushing forward the pilot reform of integrated online data processing in respect of disputes over damages in road traffic accidents. In response to the prominent problem of rapid increase and lengthy resolution procedures of disputes over traffic accidents, the Supreme People's Court initiated a comprehensive pilot project, the integrated digital database of traffic accidents disputes resolution, in Yuhang District, Hangzhou. In November 2017, the Supreme People's Court and the Ministry of Public Security, the

Ministry of Justice, and the China Insurance Regulatory Commission held a joint meeting, in which such authorities decided to jointly carry out the above- mentioned pilot reform in 14 provinces and municipalities including Beijing. The pilot integrates digital data in respect of responsibility determination by the traffic management authority, damages calculation by relevant entities, mediation, appraisal, litigation, damages paid by insurance company, and so on, and further realizes information sharing and joint actions, enabling case handled on one platform, insurance policy paid out through one click, quick processing, so as to make dispute resolution more convenient and quicker. In 2017 and 2018, nearly 370,000 and 360,000 first-instance civil disputes over damages in traffic accidents were mediated across the country respectively. In some pilot regions, through the implementation of the reform, the disputes referred to courts have dropped by 50%.

Reforming and improving the service system for civil litigations. In July 2017, the Supreme People's Court promulgated the *Certain Opinions on Further Strengthening Service in Civil Litigations* , proposing to comprehensively promote the mechanism of confirming litigants' addresses for service, to unify the format of conformation of address for service, to standardized the content of such conformation and to actively explore electronic service and effective way of preserving proof of service, in order to improve the quality and efficiency of service for civil litigations, and address the "difficulties in service" stumbling civil trials. Zhejiang Wenling People's Court has set up a service management center, equipped it with

9 full-time staff members, developed management software, opened an official WeChat account for the service management center, strengthened cooperation with postal service, and preliminarily digitalized, intensified and standardized the management of the whole process of service, thus improving the efficiency of service. Jingyang District People's Court in Deyang City, Sichuan has cut 50% of service costs through a variety of methods such as electronic service, entrusted service by notary offices, and agreements-based service, and judicial advice. Owing to the implementation of electronic service, for those cases involving insurance contracts, the duration for service has been shortened by over 5 days, and the entire trial has been shortened by over 10 days.

Enhancing the establishment of detached tribunals. In December 2014, the Supreme People's Court promulgated the *Certain Opinions on Further Strengthening the Work of Detached Tribunals in the New Context* to instruct all regions to strengthen the development of detached tribunals, in order to truly achieve the goal of exercising judicial power for the People. It has actively developed the structure of courts relying mainly on central courts and supplemented by community courts and circuit trials venues, and optimized the regional layout of people's courts and distribution of judicial personnel. The courts in Henan have established an information center, network interconnected and sharing data among all detached tribunals in the province, and developed the electronic signature system, the function of cross-regional circulation of digital case files and realized cross-county (city) filing of certain cases, enabling litigants to file cases with local courts or detached tribunals. The courts in Chongqing have pushed forward the development of tribunal liaison points and established litigation stations, in order to make the People easier filing lawsuits.

VI. Solidly Advance the "Basically Solving the Difficulties in Enforcement" Campaign

Enforcing the judgments that have come into force is the "last mile" towards judicial justice, and significantly concerns the authority and public credibility of the judiciary. In March 2016, at the 4th Session of the 12th National People's Congress, the Supreme People's Court proposed to "basically solve the difficulties in enforcement within two to three years". In April 2016, the Supreme People's Court promulgated the *Roadmap for Basically Solving the Difficulties in Enforcement within Two to Three Years*, setting the overarching goal of "basically solving the difficulties in enforcement". To achieve the goal on time, the Supreme People's Court further set five core indicators for this ongoing phase: over 90% of the cases with available property for enforcement should be enforced within the statutory period; over 90% of the cases without available property for enforcement should discontinue the enforcement in compliance with the law; over 90% of the cases with letters and visits involving enforcement should be resolved or concluded; over 90% of the courts nationwide should achieve the foregoing goals; and the overall closure rate of enforcement cases in the last three years should exceed 80%.

Since the goal of "basically solving the difficulties in enforcement" was proposed, the people's courts have comprehensively promoted the informatization and standardization, continuously deepened the reform of the system and management model of enforcement, continued to strengthen personnel capabilities, and reinforced the supports. From 2016 to the end of 2018, the courts nationwide accepted 20,435,378 enforcement cases and enforced 19,361,165 cases, with total enforced value amounting to RMB 4.4 trillion, and the year-on-year increase during this period reached 98.45%, 105.09% and 71.2% respectively.

Advancing an overarching governance structure in respect of solving the difficulties in enforcement. In June 2016, The Central Leading Group for Comprehensively Deepening Reforms (CLGCDR) considered and approved the opinions on accelerating the development of a credit- management system for the supervision over, alerting and punishing dishonest persons subject to enforcement. 31 provinces (and autonomous regions and municipalities) have issued endorsing documents, and Standing Committees of 12 Provincial, Autonomous Regional and Municipal People's Congress have promulgated the *Motions to Support the Campaign of People's Courts* . So far, the overarching governance structure for overcoming the difficulties in enforcement has emerged, featuring the leadership by the CPC party committees, coordination by CPC Political and Legal Affairs Commission, supervision by the National People's Congress, support from the local governments, organization by courts, cooperation by other corresponding authorities, and participation of the public. With continuous adjustments, this structure has laid a solid foundation for "basically solving the difficulties in enforcement".

Developing an online property search and seizure system. In response to problems such as low efficiency of enforcement, limited coverage of properties, and high human resources costs in the traditional mode of property search and seizure, the Supreme People's Court has established an online property search and seizure system at the central government level, which connects the networks of 16 central government agencies (including the Ministry of Public Security, the Ministry of Civil Affairs, the Ministry of Natural Resources, the Ministry of Transport, the People's Bank of China, and the China Banking and Insurance Regulatory Commission) and those of over 3,900 banking financial institutions. Through this system, the property information of the persons subject to enforcement officers may check has been expanded into 25 sub-categories under 16 categories, such as real estate, deposits, financial investments, vessels, vehicles, securities and online funds nationwide, which effectively covers majority of the forms of properties and related information. It greatly improves the efficiency of enforcement, and fundamentally changes the methods adopted. As of the end of 2018, the courts nationwide have searched and seized property in 60.38 million cases via this new system, with acquiring 9.84 million pieces of information of houses, lands and other forms of real estate, information of 51.42 million vehicles, 142.1 billion shares of securities, 1.939 million vessels, and RMB 25.71 billion online funds, and a total of RMB 413.6 billion frozen. Thereby, the rights and interests of the prevailing litigants are effectively safeguarded.

Improving the system of joint punishments on dishonest persons subject to enforcement. In 2013, the Supreme People's Court established the system of blacklist of dishonest persons subject to enforcement and started to promote joint punishments on dishonest persons subject to enforcement, striving to crack down on the acts of maliciously avoiding enforcements. Since 2016, the Supreme People's Court has signed memorandums with the National Development and Reform Commission and other 60 authorities, advancing a credit-management system for the supervision over, alerting and punishing dishonest persons subject to enforcement. 150 punishment measures under 37 sub-categories of 11 categories are utilized to prevent dishonest persons subject to enforcement from serving as civil servants, CPC party representatives, members to the people's congress at different levels, and members of the people's political consultative conference at different levels. They may also receive constraints in traveling, house purchasing, investing, bidding and calling for bids, and so on. As of the end of 2018, the courts nationwide had publicized 12.88 million blacklisted dishonest persons, out of which 17.46 million reservations of air tickets and 5.47 million of bullet train or high-speed rail tickets were rejected. 3.51 million dishonest persons subject to enforcement have fulfilled their obligations under such pressure.

Comprehensively promoting online judicial auctions. In order to overcome the shortcomings of conventional auction methods, the Supreme People's Court, absorbing and distilling the experiences of online judicial auctions in lower courts, has established a new judicial auction mode that online auctions are general and traditional auctions are exceptional, and promulgated judicial interpretations regarding online judicial auctions, requiring full promotion of online judicial auctions nationwide and improvement of related supporting systems from January 1, 2017. Up to now, 92.5% of the courts nationwide (namely 3,260 courts) have fully adopted online auctions, and over 80% of the judicial auctions have been conducted online. Owing to the implementation of online judicial auctions, the successful auction rate and premium rate have increased exponentially, and the rate of failed auction and price reduction as well as the auction costs has dropped significantly. Online actions effectively eliminate the rent-seeking probabilities, cut off the illegal interest chains, and bring about "zero complaint" about violation of laws and disciplines during auctions. From its launch in March 2017 to December 2018, the courts nationwide have conducted over 940,000 online auctions and thereby sold over 270,000 items for RMB 604.9 billion, with successful auction rate of 70.8% and premium rate of 64.3%, and saving commissions of RMB 18.6 billion for litigants. To tackle the low efficiency of appraisal during judicial auctions, the courts nationwide have diversified methods of appraisal such as bargaining between litigants, targeted inquiries, online inquiries and entrusted appraisals, and have established a unified online appraisal platform. With appraisals becoming more standardized and informatized, the efficiency of property disposal has been improved and the burden on litigants has been alleviated.

Improving the management of enforcements. Since 2013, the Supreme People's Court has been striving for a normative enforcement system, and has promulgated 55 judicial interpretations and regulatory documents in this regard. In particular, since 2016, 37 judicial interpretations and regulatory documents regulating property preservation, property investigation, enforcement settlement, enforcement guaranty, presupposed arbitration and other issues have been promulgated to strengthen the system, reify the rules, and effectively restrain and regulate the enforcement-related power. Since 2014, the courts nationwide have carried out a comprehensive check on the enforcement cases pending in the past 20 years, and entered over 16 million cases into the enforcement case management system, laying a solid foundation for an orderly, precise, comprehensive and intelligent management for the enforcement cases. A new mode of enforcement management has been established to put the courts at four levels nationwide in this country under "unified management, unified coordination, and unified command", transforming the management into a new flat structure being more intensified, visualized, standardized, and intelligent. A unified enforcement case handling platform has been established so that all the enforcement officers nationwide work on the same platform, harmonizing the standards and procedures for enforcement cases, and strengthening the control over key nodes. A unified enforcement command and management platform has been established. With its nearly 20 functions including enforcement coordination, property management, complaints and appeals, and proceeding supervision, this platform realized the progress that enforcement information can be publicized at "one-stop" and case handling can be pressed via "one- click". In response to the difficulties in overseeing the handling of letters and visits involving enforcement, the unified system also included all the information of letters and visits involving enforcement, through which the entire process of handling is recorded, traceable, and managed precisely.

Deepening the reform of the enforcement system and mechanisms. The pilot reform of the separation of trail power and enforcement power within the people's courts has been advanced actively and steadily. The Supreme People's Court has promulgated the *Opinions on Improving Coordination of Case Filing*, Trails and Enforcement, in order to strengthen the interactive engagements between case filing, trials, enforcement and preservation procedures. A team-based working structure has been established with judges as the team leader and legal assistants, clerks, judicial police and other auxiliary judicial personnel as the supporting members, which maximizes the utility of human resources for enforcement. The practice that property preservation applicants obtain insurance from professional insurers has been comprehensively promoted, which backs applicants struggling to provide collaterals and contributes to the increase of applications of property preservation measures. In response to the deficit of the judicial aid fund, the Supreme People's Court, on the basis of the approved pilot projects in Ningbo courts, has explored methods to expand the capital source, such as insuring the judicial assistance funds. In 2018, the granted judicial aid fund amounted to RMB 650 million.

VII. Deepening Judicial Openness and Judicial Democracy

Openness is the best means of anti-corruption. Since 2013, according to an overall integrated arrangement, by upholding to the principle of legality, voluntary, comprehensive and substantive disclosure, the Supreme People's Court has been simultaneously promoting the construction of four disclosure platforms for judicial process, court trials, written judgments, and enforcement procedures to improve judicial openness and transparency. Under the principle that disclosure is the general rule unless it meets the exceptional conditions defined by law, it has been promoting judicial openness in all areas and at all links of the trial and enforcement by the people's courts to ensure that all contents that should be disclosed and delivered to the public properly. In November 2018, the Supreme People's Court promulgated the *Opinions on Further Deepening Judicial Openness*, to continuously expand the breadth and depth of judicial openness.

Promoting the openness of judicial process. In November 2014, the China Judicial Process Information Online (https://splcgk.court.gov.cn/) was officially opened. Now, it has become a platform for centralized gathering and unified publishing of the information about the judicial process of the courts nationwide, providing "one-stop" disclosure services to the parties to the cases trialed by the courts nationwide. From the date of acceptance of a case, the parties to the case and their lawyers can, by entering their valid certificate numbers, log onto the platform to check and download the process information and documents relating to the case at any time, and receive procedural legal process online. In March 2018, the Supreme People's Court promulgated the *Provisions on the Disclosure of Judicial Process by the People's Courts through the Internet*, clarifying that, except information involving state secrets, with confidential requirement or limited access in specified by laws, all the four categories of judicial process information namely procedural information, information about other matters rising in litigation process, legal documents, and court transcripts arising from the process of trial in criminal, civil, administration and state compensation, shall be disclosed to litigants and their legal representatives, attorneys, and mandatory legal representation properly. As of the end of December 2018, the China Judicial Process Information Online had released 229,377,909 pieces of information about 4,609,074 cases, with a disclosure rate of 99.43%, and had received over 34,530,649 page views and sent 18,145,449 pieces of text messages; and on this platform, the courts nationwide had released a total of 1,536,570 pieces of information in the column "Disclosure to the Public".

Promoting the openness of court trials. On December 11, 2013, website specializing in broadcasting trials of Chinese courts went live. In September 2016, on the basis of comprehensively upgrading the Website, the Supreme People's Court officially launched the China Court Trial Online (http:// tingshen.court.gov.cn/), thereby realizing the collection and authoritative release of videos of court trials conducted at the people's courts at different levels. Since July 1, 2016, the Supreme People's Court has provided online live broadcasting of the court trials of all the cases that can be made public according to law. Through this website, the public can watch the court trials of cases that are conducted at the courts nationwide in real time, demand videos of court trials, access statistical information of court trials broadcast live, and store and share such videos and information through their Weibo and WeChat accounts, thereby realizing full coverage, real-time release and in-depth openness of court trial information. As of the end of 2018, the China Court Trial Online had broadcasted live over 2.3 million court trials with over 13.8 billion clicks. The people's courts at different levels have attached great importance to the openness of court trials of major cases and broadcast live the courts trials of a lot of major cases drawing wide attention, such as the retrial of Archangelos Gabriel salvage case and the series case of administrative disputes over "Qiaodan" trademark. On January 7-8, 2016, Haidian District People's Court in Beijing broadcast live the entire court trial of the case of "Qvodplay" suspected of seeking profits by spreading pornographic items, which lasted for more than 20 hours, attracted over 1 million viewers, and simultaneously posted 27 long Weibo messages reporting the entire court trial, which accumulatively received over 36 million views.

Promoting the openness of written judgments. In November 2013, the Supreme People's Court opened the China Judgments Online (wenshu. court.gov.cn) as the centralized platform for the openness of written judgments nationwide, and took the lead in publishing the judgments made by it on the website. Since January 1, 2014, all the effective judgments made by the people's courts at different levels have been published on the China Judgments Online. In December2015, the China Judgments Online underwent a revision by adding the functions such as one-click intelligent search, search of related documents and personalized services, and realized the openness of written judgments in five languages of minority nationalities, including Mongol, Tibetan, Uygur, Korean and Kazak, available for viewing and downloading. On August 29, 2016, the mobile client APP of the China Judgments Online was officially launched. Since August 2016, the China Judgments Online has received over 20 million page views every day. On August 29, 2016, the Supreme People's Court promulgated the amended *Provisions on the Publication of Judgments by People's Courts online*, listing all the types of judgments that should be made public, and requiring that all the judgments shall be published on line except those involving state secrets, crimes committed by persons under legal age, cases settled through mediation or in which mediation agreements are homologated, divorce actions or upbringing and guardianship of minor children; judgments involving personal privacy shall be published on line after redacting the contents involving personal privacy; the judgments of first instance that have been appealed or protested shall also be published on line and linked to the corresponding judgments of second instance; and with respect to the judgments not made public, to the extent not disclosing any state secrets, the case numbers, courts trying the cases, dates of judgment and reasons for non-disclosure shall be stated. The mode of publication of judgments has been changed from the traditional mode of centralized publication by special organs into the mode of one-click publication by the judges handling the cases on the case handling platform, and the mechanisms for handling the complaints lodged and comments made by the public and for public supervision of judgments have been established, so as to put the openness of written judgments under the supervision of all social circles. As of the end of 2018, the China Judgments Online has published over 62 million judgments, received over 21 billion page views from more than 210 countries and regions worldwide, and become the largest judgment database in the world.

Promoting the openness of enforcement information. Since November 2014, the Supreme People's Court has begun to release the information of persons subject to enforcement, the list of dishonest persons subject to enforcement by the courts nationwide, information of enforcement process and the decisions on enforcement on the China Enforcement Information Online in a centralized manner, thus realizing unified, timely, and automatic disclosure of information about enforcement cases, persons subject to enforcement, discontinued current enforcement cases, and online judicial auction, and other information of the courts nationwide. On September 14, 2016, the WeChat account of "China Enforcement" opened by the Supreme People's Court was officially launched on line, which provides the functions of access to enforcement information, publication of enforcement regulations, interpretation of laws and regulations, publication of enforcement documents, etc., so that the public can access enforcement information and receive judicial services anytime anywhere. As of the end of 2018, the enforcement information release platform had announced 12.88

million dishonest persons subject to enforcement.

Promoting the disclosure of corporate bankruptcy information. In August 2016, the Supreme People's Court published the *Provisions on Disclosure of Information about Corporate Bankruptcy Cases* , and officially opened the National Enterprise Bankruptcy and Restructuring Case Information Disclosure Platform, which becomes an online information platform for releasing various information about bankruptcy cases complying with different levels, and on which the legal process, notices of recruitment of administrators, notices of recruitment of investors, notices of asset auction and other relevant information are simultaneously published, so as to provide services for the creditors, enterprises in debt, market investors and other interested parties. In 2018, the information about 29,856 bankruptcy cases was disclosed through the National Enterprise Bankruptcy Information Disclosure Platform.

Expanding the breadth and depth of judicial openness. The Supreme People's Court has published the *Gazettes of the Supreme People's Court*, *Work Reports of the Supreme People's Court* and the *Annual Work Reports of the People's Court* (in Chinese and English) on a regular basis, as well as the white papers on the situation of judicial protection of intellectual property rights in China, on the trial of maritime cases, on the trial of environmental and resource cases, on the trial of administrative cases, on the judicial reform and on the judicial openness, and released the judicial documents and information about major cases and the work of courts to people at home and abroad. The Supreme People's Court has established the

Judicial Case Academy and opened the Online version (https://anli.court. gov.cn/static/web/index.html#/index), which, supported by the big database and the Information Technology, collects and publishes a large number of Chinese and foreign cases, and intelligently produces typical cases widely recognized, thus promoting clear and defined guides to the society. The China Judicial Case Academy Online with columns such as "Hot Issues", "Case Method" and "Case Forum", has been leading the legal practitioners to participate in the collection, generation, research and communication on judicial cases, striving to become a new platform for case studies. The people's courts at different levels have been making efforts to improve judicial openness by means of court official websites and accounts, Court Weibo and WeChat, mobile news client APPs, court president's letterboxes, liaison platforms of members of people's congresses and people's political consultative conferences, open days with themes and otherwise.

On December 31, 2014, the governmental service website of the Supreme People's Court underwent a comprehensive revision and opened the litigation service website to facilitate consultations, inquiries, appointment for case filing, online examination of case files and contact with judges for the litigants, among other things. On December 15, 2015, the Supreme People's Court opened its English website. Since 2013, the Supreme People's Court has opened its official accounts on the major domestic Weibo platforms including Sina Weibo, Tencent Weibo and Renmin Weibo platforms, and press rooms for the courts nationwide on such Weibo accounts. As of the end of 2018, the three official Weibo accounts owned over 57.953 million subscribers, posted 44,000 pieces of Weibo messages, 5.084 million of which received reposts and comments. The official WeChat account of the Supreme People's Court went live in November 2013, and had posted 3,909 pieces of image-text messages and had 1,044,000 subscribers as of the end of 2018. Since January 2015, the courts nationwide have adopted the Monthly Updates Press system. From 2014 to 2018, the Supreme People's Court had held 114 news presses, published 76 judicial documents and circulated 53 reports on working progress. From 2015 to 2018, 477 typical cases in total have been made public through briefings on typical cases. The Supreme People's Court held the China-ASEAN Justice Forum, the BRICS Justice Forum and the Environmental Justice Sub-forum of Boao Forum for Asia, the Conference of Presidents of Supreme Courts of China and Central and Eastern European Countries, the Silk Road (Dunhuang) International Forum on Judicial Cooperation, the Forum on the Rule of Law in Cyberspace – Smart Court, the Conference of Presidents of Supreme Courts of China and Portuguese-speaking Countries, and the 13th Conference of Presidents of Supreme Courts of the Member States of the Shanghai Cooperation Organization, and other major events of foreign affairs related to justice. It has established friendly relations with the highest judicial authorities of over 140 countries and regions, 18 international and regional organizations and has signed cooperation agreements with the highest judicial authorities of 43 countries and 2 international organizations; in doing so, it has told a story about the rule of law in China well and transmitted the sound of the rule of law in China, effectively enhancing the international image and influence of China's judiciary.

Reforming the system of people's assessors. In May 2015, with the authorization of the Standing Committee of the National People's Congress, the Supreme People's Court and the Ministry of Justice jointly promulgated the pilot program to reform the system of people's assessors and the measures for the implementation of the pilot program. The two-year pilot program has been conducted at 50 courts selected in 10 provinces, autonomous regions and municipalities. The items of the pilot program includes, among other things, reforming the requirements for the appointment of People's Assessors, improving the mode of appointment of People's Assessors, expanding the scope of participation in trials, defining the powers to participate in trials, enhancing job security, establishing the withdrawal mechanism, giving full play to the advantage of People's Assessors in being familiar with the social situations and public opinions, and gradually realizing the goal that People's Assessors no longer vote on issues relating to the application of law and only participate in the finding of facts. In order to further address the problems arising in the pilot reform, in April 2017, the Standing Committee of the National People's Congress decided to extend the pilot period by one year. In April 2018, the Standing Committee of the National People's Congress considered and passed the report of the Supreme People's Court on the pilot reform of the system of People's Assessors, which was successfully completed. The pilot reform has achieved remarkable accomplishments, including "four conversions": the appointment of People's Assessors has transformed from mainly relied on recommendations by social organizations to random selection; the scope of the discretionary power of People's Assessors' in trials has been narrowed down from full participation to only factual issues; the maximum number of People's Assessors in a Collegiate Panel has been enlarged from3 to more than 7; and the evaluative assessment on the cases heard with the People's Assessors has shifted from "quantity" to "quality". After the reform, the People's Assessors come from more diverse backgrounds with a sound structure, and fulfill their responsibilities more actively. In April 2018, the *Law on People's Assessors of the People's Republic of China* was promulgated, legally incorporated the improvements in the pilot reform of the system of People's Assessors. The Ministry of Justice, the Supreme People's Court, and the Ministry of Public Security issued measures for appointment of People's Assessors, and established the appointment of People's Assessors mainly based on random selection and with supplement methods of individual applications and organization recommendations.

VIII. Promoting Scientific and Classified Management over Judicial Personnel

According to the overall arrangement by the State and in cooperation with related departments of the Central Government, the Supreme People's Court has fully reformed the judicial personnel management system by cooperating with related departments of the Central Government in improving the classified management over the personnel of the courts, reforming the selection and appointment of the judges, implementing the judge quota system, establish the system on the independent rank of posts and compensation system of the judges.

Establishing a system for classified management of judicial personnel. In response to the problem that the past judicial personnel management system did not fully reflect the characteristics of the judicial profession, the Supreme People's Court has actively promoted the reform of the system for classified management of judicial personnel, by classifying the judicial personnel into judges, auxiliary judicial personnel and judicial administrative personnel, and adopting different management systems for different categories of personnel, to ensure that each of judges, auxiliary judicial personnel and judicial administrative personnel is assigned to a definite post of duty and attends to his own duties. As of the end of 2018, the proportion of judges, auxiliary judicial personnel and judicial administrative personnel had reached 34.6%, 49.5% and 15.9% respectively.

Fully implementing the judge quota system. In line with the principle of determining quota based on cases, selecting personnel based on job requirements, controlling total number, and making overall planning at the provincial level, through well-designed examination and assessment procedures, the courts nationwide have selected a total of 125,000 judges from the former 210,000 judges. The newly-selected judges are mainly placed on adjudicative posts rather than general administrative posts, and over 85% of judicial personnel resources are allocated to trial work, optimized the resource allocation and the team structure. All higher people's courts have strictly honored the maximum quota and ratio determined by the Central Government, and according to the number of cases handled, and the situations of economic and social development, population and other basic figures of the places where the courts are located, the level of trial and functions of the courts, workloads of judges, staffing of auxiliary judicial personnel and other factors, have implemented a system of unified allocation of judge quota among the courts at three levels within one provincial jurisdiction and providing priority to the primary people's courts and the area where the conflicts between caseload and personnel are serious. Mainly on the amount of cases, Guangdong courts decided that the proportion of judges should be lower than 30% in Shantou where there are fewer cases but overmuch staffs, and be higher than 50% in Shenzhen, Dongguan, Zhongshan and other cities where there are overloaded cases but relatively fewer staffs. A mechanism of exchange and removal of judges has been established, and a mechanism of dynamic management of quota has been gradually formed, whereby one may be appointed or removal as judge and an appointed judge may be promoted or demoted. As of June 2018, 5,938 judges nationwide have been removed due to post transfer, reassignment, resignation, retirement, and disqualification, or the like.

Reforming the judge selection and appointment system. The courts at the provincial level have established judge selection committees comprising judge representatives and relevant civilians, and formulated open, fair and just judge selection and appointment procedures, to ensure that only outstanding legal practitioners who are upright in character and have rich experience and a high professional level will become judge candidates. In order to improve the system of selection of judges level by level, in May 2016, the Organization Department of the CCCPC, the Supreme People's Court and the Supreme People's Procuratorate jointly promulgated the *Opinions on Establishing the System of Selection of Judges and Public Prosecutors Level by Level*, which expressly provides that the judges of the people's courts at the prefecture level or above shall be selected level by level generally. In October 2015, the Supreme People's Court, after strict selection procedures, selected 7 outstanding judges from 62 applicants from local courts nationwide. In March 2014, the Supreme People's Court conducted a program of publicly selecting high-level judicial talents from experts, scholars, lawyers and other personnel practicing law, and finally selected five persons, including experts, scholars, senior lawyers and outstanding public prosecutors, from 195 applicants. In 2015, the courts in

Shanghai publicly selected one judge from outside the judicature, and the courts in Qinghai publicly selected three judges from outside the judicature. The courts in Shanghai, Guangdong, Fujian and other regions have begun to select judges from outstanding judge assistants and send them to serve in the primary people's courts.

Reforming the rank of posts and compensation & benefit system of judges. A system of independent rank of posts of judges has been established so that: registered judges could be managed according to such independent ranking order, judges' professional ranks are separated from their administrative ranks, and judges are promoted based on their seniority, on a selective basis or specially; a personnel management system for judges that is different from that for other public servants and reflects the professional characteristics of judges has been implemented, which will broaden the career development channels of grassroots judges and enhance the professional honor and work enthusiasm of judges. As of the end of 2018, all courts nationwide had established a mechanism for determining the independent rank of posts of judges, about 98% courts had begun to promote judges along with their seniority, and about 52% courts had begun to promote judges on a selective basis. A compensation & benefit system has been established, supporting the series of reforms of independent rank of posts of judges, and all courts nationwide have introduced the new salary system involving performance-based bonus, which greatly increased the salary level of judges. By actively coordinating with related departments of the Central Government, the Supreme People's Court has formulated policies on post exchange, retirement age, medical benefit, travel allowance, traffic subsidy, and others benefits for judges, noticed those implementation of policies, and promoted the courts at different levels to effectively place these policies.

Reforming the system of recruiting and training auxiliary judicial personnel. The Supreme People's Court, in cooperation with related departments of the Central Government, has promulgated *Opinion on Recruiting Judge Assistants by People's Courts*. All regions have conducted unified independent recruitment at provincial level in an orderly way, and steadily advanced the position transfer of judges that are not in the judge quota system and qualified clerks to judge assistant, to equip the courts with more judge assistants. In April 2017, the Supreme People's Court, together with the Ministry of Finance and the Ministry of Human Resources and Social Security, promulgated a *Plan for Reforming the System on Managing Clerks*, with a focus on the problems solving that the management of contracted clerks was not standardized enough, the professional protection provided to contracted clerks is not strong enough, and the team of contracted clerks is not stable enough. The courts in all regions have expanded the sources of auxiliary judicial personnel and explored the improvement of the system on managing and training auxiliary judicial personnel, with a focus on optimizing the structure of auxiliary judicial personnel. Since the reform, the number of auxiliary judicial personnel in Beijing courts has increased 68.8% from 2,689 to 4,538; the ratio of number of judges to that of auxiliary judicial personnel in Shanghai courts has changed from 1:0.75 to 1:1.78. The Jiangsu Higher People's Court has vigorously pushed forward the reform of the clerk system, formulated the standards of the rank of posts of clerks and measures for the training and evaluating clerks, properly defined the posts, the quantity and responsibilities of clerks, and provided that the proportion of first-line judges to clerks shall be 1:1.1, thereby changing the situation that several judges assisted by one clerk in the past.

Establishing the legal research scholar and legal intern systems. The Supreme People's Court has established legal research scholar and intern systems, and received 30 legal research scholars and 313 legal interns, which enhances its judicial cooperation and exchanges with law schools and research institutes, and improves the legal practitioner cultivating mechanism. Most local courts have enhanced their cooperation with law schools and established a system of receiving interns from law schools as judge assistants, who participate in the auxiliary judicial work under the guidance of judges, alleviated the difficulty of understaffed judge assistants in the people's courts, and explored a new mode of classified management of judicial personnel. Chengdu Intermediate People's Court in Sichuan has signed a cooperation agreement on a mechanism of "Judge Assistant Internship" with 11 colleges and universities including Sichuan University, Southwestern University of Finance and Economics and University of Electronic Science and Technology of China, by launching a program of intern judge assistants on campuses, whereby the colleges and universities in cooperation could select and send outstanding law graduates (or undergraduates) to participate in the auxiliary judicial work. So far, a total of 304 interns of five phases have engaged in this program.

Strengthening the professional ethics of the judiciary. In order to comprehensively strengthen the professional quality of judges and abide by the professional ethics of the judiciary, the people's courts have improved the unified vocational training system and entry/promotion oath ceremony and the professional ethics standards, code of professional conduct and professional ethics evaluation mechanism for judges. In conjunction with the related departments of the Central Government, the Supreme People's Court has issued the relevant documents, prohibiting judicial personnel from entering into six ways of intercommunications with litigants, lawyers, specially interested parties or agencies, requiring judicial personnel handling cases to host litigants, lawyers, especially interested parties or agencies at working places and during working hours, and prohibiting judicial personnel from acting as attorneys or mandatory legal representation in any cases handled by the judicial organs he resigned, and prohibiting those from practicing law for life who have been dismissed from public office due to violation of the law and discipline.

IX. Improving the System and Mechanism of Judicial Service and Securing National Development

The people's courts shoulder an important mission for protecting the political security of the country, ensuring the stability of the overall society, defending social fairness and justice, and guaranteeing that People live and work in peace and satisfaction. Based on their judicial functions, the people's courts at different levels have deepened the reform of the judicial system by strengthening adjudication and enforcement, to promote the formation of a new pattern of reform and opening-up at higher lever and create a more stable, fair, transparent and predictable business environment under the rule of law.

Enabling the mechanism of judicial service and protection for the national development strategy. The Supreme People's Court has issued documents on providing judicial protection for improving the business environment under the rule of law. Higher People's Courts of Beijing and Shanghai have also improved relevant judicial policies, committed to create an international environment for doing business under the rule of law. In the *Doing Business 2019* released by the World Bank, China scored 78.97 in the indicator of "performing contract", which indicator is ranked the 6th in the world, and closely related to the judicial efficiency, judicial cost, judicial organ, judicial procedure and informatization level. The Supreme

People's Court has promulgated the *Opinions on Providing Judicial Service and Protection for the Coordinated Development of Beijing-Tianjin-Hebei Region, the Development of the Yangtze River Economic Belt, and the Rural Revitalization Strategy*, and has innovated the judicial collaborative working mechanism, to provide judicial service and protection for the major strategic development of the country. It has improved the risk monitoring and warning mechanism in financial adjudication, established a big database for financial cases, and improved the information sharing and distribution mechanism for preventing financial risk.

Improving the international commercial dispute resolution mechanism in relation to "The Belt and Road" Initiative. In June 2018, the Supreme People's Court promulgated several judicial interpretations on the establishment of international commercial courts, and formulated supporting rules such as working rules for international commercial expert committees and guidelines on procedures of international commercial courts. The international commercial courts may entrust members of International Commercial Expert Committees and International Commercial Mediation Agency to mediate international commercial disputes, and support domestic qualified arbitration institutions with international reputation in carrying out international commercial arbitration involving "The Belt and Road" Initiative, so as to create a system for diversified resolution mechanism of international commercial disputes with interconnected and supportive mediation, arbitration and litigation. On June 29, 2018, the First International Commercial Court and Second International Commercial

Court of the Supreme People's Court were established and officially opened in Shenzhen and Xi'an respectively.

Improving the system of judicial protection of property rights. In November 2016, the Supreme People's Court promulgated the *Opinions on Fulfilling the Role and Function of the Judiciary to Effectively Strengthen the Judicial Protection of Property Rights* and made comprehensive arrangements for improving the judicial protection of property rights. By upholding the concepts of equal, comprehensive and legitimate protection, the people's courts ensure that all types of property right owners should be given equal treatment on legal status and law application, strictly distinguish economic disputes from criminal offences, and resolutely prevent transferring civil obligations to criminal offences. The Supreme People's Court has published two batches of typical cases regarding protection of property rights and entrepreneurs' rights and interests, and has legally identified and corrected some property-right-related cases in which people are unjust, falsely or wrongly charged or sentenced, such as Zhang Wenzhong case, which has good social impacts.

Strengthening the reform and innovation in IP adjudications. In November 2017, at the first session of the 19th CLGCDR, the CLGCDR members reviewed and approved the *Opinions on Certain Issues Concerning Strengthening the Reform and Innovation in Adjudication of IP Cases*, and proposed to improve the IP judicial system by improving the examination mechanism and evidence rules on of validity of rights in line with the characteristics of IP adjudication and establishing a compensation rules based on marketing value for IP infringement. On April 20, 2017, the Supreme People's Court promulgated *Outlines of Judicial Protection of Intellectual Property Rights in China (2016-2020)*, which clarifies the basic principles, main objectives and key measures for judicial protection of intellectual property rights. In July 2016, the Supreme People's Court promulgated the *Opinions on Promoting Three-in-one Trial of Civil, Administrative and Criminal IP Cases at the Courts Nationwide*, requiring that the IP adjudication divisions of all the people's courts at different levels shall be renamed the IP tribunals, which shall be in charge of the trial of all the civil, administrative and criminal IP cases.

Improving the system and mechanism of judicial protection for ecological resources. The Supreme People's Court has issued documents to provide judicial protection for comprehensively promoting the ecological civilization construction and greenness development. All regions have strengthened the establishment of specialized judicial organs for environmental and resource cases. In June 2014, the Supreme People's Court established the Environmental and Resource Tribunal. As of the end of December 2018, 22 higher people's courts, 110 intermediate people's courts and 257 grassroots people's courts had established specialized judicial organs for environmental and resource cases; the courts nationwide had established 1,270 tribunals, collegiate panels and circuit tribunals for environmental and resource cases in total, including 390 tribunals, 808 collegiate panels, and 72 circuit tribunals. As required by the plan for pilot reform of ecological damage compensation system, all regions have actively explored adjudication rules for a provincial government to bring claims for ecological damages. As of 2018, the courts nationwide had accepted and handled 20 cases claiming for and judicial homologation of ecological damage compensation.

X. Improving the Judicial Management System and the Jurisdiction System

Since 2014, in cooperation with related departments of the Central Government, the Supreme People's Court has promoted the reform of judicial management system, adjusted the jurisdiction system, improved the system for safeguarding the authority of judicature, and facilitated the creation of a favorable institutional and social environment trusting, respecting and supporting judicature.

Promoting centralized management of personnel, financial and material resources of local courts below provincial level. The reform of the judicial management system by promoting centralized management of personnel, financial and material resources of local courts below the provincial level reflects that the judicial power is a power of the Central Government in nature. All the regions have advanced the work of centralized management in an open, transparent and democratic manner relying on the provincial platforms. The size and composition of local courts below provincial level in a provincial-level region are subject to management by the provincial commission department with the assistance of the higher people's court in that region. The commission departments at municipal or county level are no longer responsible for the management of size and composition of courts within their respective jurisdictions. Each provincial-level region has the mechanism that the judges of local courts below provincial level are subject to nomination, management, appointment and removal according to the legal procedures by the provincial-level government in a centralized manner. Judge assistants are recruited and employed by provincial-level public server management departments in conjunction with higher people's courts in a centralized manner. Junior judges are subject to professional qualification examination by provincial-level judge selection committees, and nomination, appointment and removal according to the legal procedures by provincial-level governments in a centralized manner.

The provincial-level regions have also explored the reform of centralized funding management system for local courts below provincial level in light of their respective local conditions. In 18 provinces, autonomous regions and municipalities such as Beijing, Tianjin and Shanxi and 2 cities specifically designated by the state plan namely Dalian and Shenzhen, the funds required by local courts below provincial level are managed in a unified way by the provincial level, and all the courts at the provincial, municipal and county levels are classified as first-level budgetary units and prepare and submit their respective budgets to the provincial-level financial departments; their budgetary funds are appropriated from the central payment system of the Treasury.

Improving the trial-level system. In order to adapt to the situations of economic and social development, and reasonably defining the respective functions of the courts at four levels, the Supreme People's Court adjusted the thresholds for the jurisdiction of the higher people's courts and intermediate people's courts over civil and commercial cases of first instance, and increased the threshold of the subject value of civil and commercial cases of first instance under the jurisdiction of grassroots people's courts; provided that major, difficult and complicated cases, new types of cases and typical cases in terms of application of law may be adjudicated by a people's court at a higher level as determined by it in its sole discretion or at the request of a people's court at a lower level. In February 2015, the Supreme People's Court promulgated the judicial interpretations on issues concerning strict application of order for retrial and remand for retrial in the supervisory procedure for the trial of civil cases, which unify the standard for order for retrial and review of cases, strictly prohibit remand for retrial at will, and request that if a people's court at a higher level orders to retry a case or remand a case for retrial, it shall elaborate in the ruling the detailed reasons for such order for retrial or remand for retrial.

Conducting pilot reform of trans-regional centralized jurisdiction over administrative cases. Considering that an administrative case is subject to jurisdiction of the court in the place where the administrative organ as the defendant is located and may be subject to interference by local administrative organs, according to the overall arrangement by the Central Government, the courts in all regions have been exploring the establishment of a system of jurisdiction over administrative cases relatively separate from administrative divisions, through escalation of the jurisdiction to the higher level, cross-jurisdiction among different regions, relatively centralized jurisdiction and otherwise, carrying out reforms of the jurisdiction system with different characteristics, to practically solve serious problems in administrative lawsuits, such as difficulty in case filing, difficulty in trial and difficulty in enforcement. In June 2015, the Supreme People's Court promulgated the *Opinions on Trans-regional Centralized Jurisdiction over Administrative Cases*, instructing certain higher people's courts to, according to their respective local conditions, designate some courts to exercise jurisdiction over trans-regional administrative cases, so as to integrate resources of administrative adjudication and improve the judicial environment for administrative adjudication. The higher people's courts in Fujian, Shandong, Henan, Guangdong, Hubei, Hunan and other provinces and regions assigned the jurisdiction over certain administrative cases of first instance to some designated primary or intermediate people's courts other than the courts originally having the jurisdiction over such cases, so as to eliminate the public's concern about local protectionism, through fairly adjudicating all kinds of administrative cases as per law.

Improving the system of specialized adjudication of and centralized jurisdiction over environmental and resource cases. The courts at different levels have been exploring the mode of specialized adjudication of civil, administrative and criminal environmental and resource cases. The Environmental and Resource Tribunal of the Supreme People's Court hear and adjudicate civil and administrative environmental and resource cases in a centralized manner. 16 higher people's courts such as those in Jiangsu and Fujian hear and adjudicate civil and administrative environmental and resource cases or civil, administrative and criminal environmental and resource cases in a centralized manner. The courts in all regions have been exploring the mode of centralized jurisdiction over trans-regional environmental and resource cases, based on the characteristics of environmental and resources protection in each region. The higher people's courts in Jiangsu, Henan, Hainan, Hubei and other provinces and regions have been exploring the centralized jurisdiction over environmental and resource cases within each of the ecosystems or ecological functional zones such as river basins and sea areas, and have been exploring the jurisdiction and adjudication mode more matching the characteristics of the ecological environment laws, to effectively prevent local protectionism and enhance ecological environmental protection.

Strengthening the system requiring principals of administrative organs to appear in the court to respond to charges in accordance with the law. In July 2016, the Supreme People's Court issued a *Notice Requiring the People's Courts in All Regions* to further regulate and promote response to administrative lawsuits pursuant to the relevant provisions of *the Administrative Procedure Law of the People's Republic of China*, and providing that if the principal or related staff members of an administrative organ do not appear in the court personally and just appoint an attorney to appear in the court, or if the principal of an administrative organ fails to appear in the court at the written request of the people's court, the people's court shall record the fact in the case file and state it in the judgment, and may issue public notices thereon according to law, and suggest that the appointing authority, supervisory authority or the administrative organ at the higher level should impose serious punishments on the responsible persons. In Jiangsu Province, the rate of appearance of principals of administrative organs in the court to respond to charges has remained above 90% for two consecutive years, in particular, the rate of their appearance in the court has been above 90% in Nantong and other eight prefecture-level cities, and reached 100% in Kunshan and other 58 counties (cities and districts); while in Hai'an County, the three consecutive heads of the County have appeared in the court to respond to charges and the rate of appearance of principals of administrative organs in the court to respond to charges has remained 100% for six consecutive years.

Improving the system for safeguarding the credibility of lawsuits and the authority of judicature. The Supreme People's Court, in conjunction with the Standing Committee of the National People's Congress, amended certain charges under the Criminal Law, to further safeguard the authority of judicature. *The Ninth Amendment to the Criminal Law of the People's Republic of China* adopted on August 29, 2015 further defined the offences of refusal to execute judgments or rulings, added an offence under the Criminal Law and inserted the provisions regarding offences committed by entities; amended the offences of interference with court order by defining the acts of beating up the parties to lawsuits, or insulting, defaming or threatening the judicial personnel or parties to lawsuits, or refusing to obey the court's order to stop such acts or otherwise seriously interfering with court order as offences; and added the offences of false charges by defining the acts of bringing any civil lawsuit on the ground of fabricated facts, disturbing the judicial order or otherwise seriously damaging the legitimate rights and interests of others as offences. In June 2016, the Supreme People's Court promulgated the *Guidelines on Preventing and Punishing the Persons Lodging False Charges*, instructing the courts in all regions to identify the elements of false charges, and enhance the examination of and punishment against false charges, to safeguard the credibility and order of lawsuits.

XI. Advancing the Construction of Intelligent Courts

Since 2013, the people's courts have conscientiously implemented the innovation-driven strategy, the national cyber development strategy, the big data strategy, and the new-generation artificial intelligence development plan, and comprehensively strengthened the construction of intelligent courts. The open, and intelligent online Apps have been comprehensively developed, and the main framework of court informatization version 3.0 has been established, which greatly promotes the modernization of the judicial system and judicial capability.

Enhancing the formulation of top-level informatization planning and standards. The Supreme People's Court has issued the *Five Year Development Plan on Informatization of People's Courts 2016-2020*, clarifying the key tasks and specific requirements for the construction of intelligent courts. In accordance with the guidelines of "systematic projects, standards first", the Supreme People's Court has improved the system of standards for informatization of the people's courts, developed and released 85 technical standards focus on the case data standards, to support the information resource sharing and exchange, system R&D, information security and high quality and efficiency operation and maintenance system construction. It has promulgated certain provisions on the *Numbers of Cases Handled by People's Courts and Supplementary Standards*, the *Case*

Information Standard for People's Courts (2015) and other normative documents to implement code-based management of 3,500 courts nationwide, built a three-level case types system, thereby laying a solid foundation for building a new standard system for case information.

Strengthening the construction of informatization infrastructure and security system. The courts at different levels have been constantly upgrading and improving the court network systems to support online handling of all judicial matters, including private court network, mobile network, private external network, confidential intranets and Internet. Over 3,500 courts and over 10,000 detached tribunals across the country have connected with the private court network. Over 28,000 scientific and technological courtrooms have been established nationwide to realize multimedia evidence demonstration, remote trial, audio and video recording of court trials, and automated voice recognition in process, and other functions. The Supreme People's Court took the lead in proposing and establishing a high quality and efficiency operation and maintenance guarantee system, and building and using visualized operation and maintenance management tools, which horizontally cover the five major network systems, vertically run through five layers, namely infrastructure, judicial application, data management, information security, and operation & maintenance.

Fully promoting electronic litigation. For further development in the Internet era, to promote the innovation of litigation mode and mechanism, the courts at different levels have been vigorously promoting electronic litigation for whole-process online. The Supreme People's Court has been instructing and promoting the courts nationwide to deploy five online standard modules for case filing, payment, evidence exchange, hearing, and electronic documents service. The courts in Jilin, Zhejiang, and Jiangsu have fully established and widely used these modules. Zhejiang took the lead in piloting in Ningbo and promoting across the province "Mobile WeCourt", an one-step mobile litigation platform on WeChat small procedures, which enables the litigants handles more than 20 judicial matters online, such as case filing, inquiry, mediation, court trial, enforcement and payment. Mobile WeCourt has reduced the average time consumption for the courts in Ningbo, Zhejiang Province to adjudicate first-instance civil and commercial cases by 17 days, the average time consumption to enforce by 28 days, and the figures of litigants' complaints on "judges are often too busy to contact" by nearly 30%.

Developing and applying a criminal trial intelligent assistant system. According to the Central Government's plan for pushing forward the reform of the trial-centered litigation system, Shanghai has developed a criminal trial intelligent assistant system with high-techs such as big data, cloud computing, and artificial intelligence to formulate uniformly evidence standards applicable and evidence rules and embed them in the criminal case handling system of public security organs, procuratorial organs, courts, and judicial administrative organs, so as to help staff on duty to collect and examine evidence in a legal, comprehensive, and standardized manner, and ensure that the facts of cases found during investigations, prosecutions and trials are legitimate and that the whole process of handling criminal cases should be visualized, recorded and supervised, so as to reduce the arbitrariness of the judiciary and effectively prevent the occurrence of unjust, falsely or wrongly charged or sentenced cases.

Strengthening the intelligent assistance in case trial and judicial management. In August 2016, the Supreme People's Court promulgated *Guiding Opinions on Comprehensively Promoting the Simultaneous Generation and In-depth Application of Electronic Case Files by People's Courts*, for the purpose of promoting the electronic archiving of case files and the uploading to the case handling system, creating conditions for online case- handling and the intelligent assistance in case trial for judges. Relying on the big data management and service platform, the Supreme People's Court has generated the information about cases files of courts nationwide, which lays the technical foundation for a court to access the electronic case files of another court. The Supreme People's Court has established the "Faxin" platform to build a world-class legal information service, gather various academic resources, cases, professional practices and improvements, and provide comprehensive, convenient and intelligent service for searching and delivering legal acknowledge resource to different groups such as judges, legal professionals, scholars and the public. All regions have developed a voice recognition system for trials, which can automatically transform voice into texts. Suzhou Intermediate People's Court in Jiangsu has implemented the system to support over 27,000 court-hearings, with accuracy rate of voice recognition above 90%, and with which trial time shortened by 20%-30% on average.

Having informatization and big data serve judicial management and decision making. The Supreme People's Court has built a big database to collect, manage, and analyze the judicial information from the courts nationwide and provide information services in need. This big database collects the information about the case acceptance and closure by the courts nationwide in real time, automatically updates such information every 5 minutes, and collects information about 70,000 to 80,000 cases every day. It is now the world's largest database of judicial information and supports the analysis on the information about case acceptance and closure by the courts nationwide and the distribution of cause of action of these cases. In 2016, the courts nationwide fully realized the integration of judicial statistics with the big data management and service platform, which indicates that the people's courts have completely ended the history of manual justice statistics. As needed by the quantitative personnel performance evaluation, the big data management and service platform connects and integrates the collected personnel data and case data, puts forward the central method of judicial personnel management shifting from qualitative to quantitative.

Conclusion

The new round of the reform of judicial system has been both problem-oriented and goal-oriented, starting from the deep-seated problems affecting judicial fairness and inhibiting judicial capability, and the problems involving the direct and realistic interests that the public concern most; such reform has been observing all the time the laws of justice while proceeding from China's actual conditions, exploring the road of reform of the judicial system with Chinese characteristics, focusing on building and improving the socialist judicial system with Chinese characteristics, and has been pushed forward step by step law, and combined top-layer design with exploration through pilot programs, so as to ensure that the reform will be conducted in a vigorous and steady manner.

The People's understanding and support are the driving force behind the judicial reform, and the People's sense of gain is the standard for evaluating the judicial reform. In light of the new challenges in the new era, the People's new expectations and new progress in science and technology, the judicial reform of Chinese courts will always be pushed forward and never be finished. In the next step, the people's courts will, follow the guidance of Xi Jinping Thought on Socialism with Chinese Characteristics for a New Era, hold highly the great banner of reform and opening up in the new era, and unremittingly pursue the goal to make the public experience fairness and justice in each judicial case, make the fair, efficient and authoritative socialist judicial system with Chinese characteristics more mature and well-established, comprehensively improve the competency, efficiency and credibility of the judiciary, create a better environment for socialist rule of law, advance the judicial civilization to a higher level, and strive to make the People obtain fair and just outcomes in every judicial case.